BRING JADE HOME

The True Story of a Dog Lost in Yellowstone

Michelle Caffrey

*"Not just for dog lovers; a passionate reminder of the wonders
of Yellowstone and its inhabitants at a time
when our national parks are being threatened."*
—Kirkus Reviews

ISBN: 978-1-56037-735-1

Yellowstone overview map by David Sowers.
Reunion photos courtesy of Patti Johnson and Elena Torphy.
All others by David Sowers and Laura Gillice.

Front cover photo of Jade by Caitlin Ascher.
Inset photos: Grizzly bear and bull elk, Jim Peaco, NPS; gray wolf, Jacob W. Frank, NPS;
mountain lion, Sumio Harada.

Editor Beverly A. Jackson.

For more information about our books, write Farcountry Press,
P.O. Box 5630, Helena, MT 59604; call (800) 821-3874; or visit
www.farcountrypress.com.

Library of Congress Cataloging-in-Publication data on file.

 Produced and printed in the United States of America.

22   21   20   19   18   1   2   3   4   5

||||||||||||||||||||||||||||||||||||||||||||||||||||||||||||||||||||||||||||||||||||||||||||||||||

To Kat Brekken and all those who searched for Jade

||||||||||||||||||||||||||||||||||||||||||||||||||||||||||||||||||||||||||||||||||||||||||||||||||

According to www.crystalvaults.com,
Blue jade is a talisman of peace and serenity.
It calms and restores, like a veil of
slow moving clouds coverng the moon...
and is widely used to temper emotional upheaval
and to restore equilibrium.

Contents |||||||||||||||||||||||||||||

YELLOWSTONE NATIONAL PARK

Kat Brekken's Home

Ice Lake Trailhead

Wreck Site

Canyon Village Meadows

Norris Geyser Basin

Wreck Site

Wreck Site

Canyon Village

Carcass Dump

Old Faithful

Grand Canyon of the Yellowstone

Chapter One

A VACATION FOR THE DOGS

JULY 23—Yellowstone National Park is a paradise of mountain wilderness, studded with dramatic canyons, alpine rivers, and lush forests. David Sowers knew just below the earth's crust seethed an enormous hot spot of magma—a supervolcano. His geologist father had taught him if it were to erupt, as it has at least three times in the distant past, it would be a catastrophic end to life as we know it.

That particular day, however, David was more interested in his new girlfriend Laura Gillice and their dogs than the remote possibility of an impending, life-changing disaster.

After taking their two Australian shepherds for a walk along the Canyon to Norris road, he started loading them into the back of his Nissan Xterra. He easily led Laura's ten-month-old puppy Laila into her metal crate. Now the problem child. He turned his attention to his black and white fifteen-month-old dog Jade. She regarded him with azure eyes and wagged her stubbed tail, resulting in a furious rear end wiggle.

"Shake it don't break it, Jade." He tried to cajole her into her plastic airline carrier. "Come on girl. We're going someplace fun, not the vet. Don't be a...." She resisted, pulling hard on the leash. He tried a stern voice and since he rarely used it, hoped it would have an effect on his dog. After several minutes of a battle of wills, she was finally in her crate.

He hopped into the passenger side and slammed the door shut. "Well that was easy."

Laura laughed. "Lure her with a treat. You'll be more successful training her." It had been her idea to crate the dogs on their first trip together. Jade usually rode in the front seat with David. It was too dangerous, Laura reasoned. She knew firsthand how the unexpected could happen and it didn't hurt to be prepared.

"Jade's the one training *me*," he admitted. No doubt, she had a mind of her own. Recently he'd put up a wooden fence around his property. Jade took one glance and easily jumped it. She returned when she chose to, ignoring his calls. On the drive up from Denver, Jade had barked about every two hours as if she needed to pee. After a few unnecessary stops, he'd realized she'd been playing him.

Laura glanced at her phone, studying the photo David had just taken of her at Yellowstone Falls. She posed where she'd once been photographed as a five-year old.

"Is that what you wanted?" David leaned over, placing a hand on her bare knee.

"It'll be perfect for Throwback Thursday." The image fifty years later was of a tall, fit blonde smiling confidently into the camera. Jade and Laila barked and Laura laughed as she started the engine. "This vacation is for the dogs."

"You're right, darlin.' They're lucky puppies." His endearment always brought out his Amarillo, Texas drawl even though he'd lived in Colorado most of his life.

Inhaling the scent of pine through the open window, Laura steered along the highway as heavy tourist traffic whizzed by. Glancing at the dashboard clock, she noted it read a few minutes after three in the afternoon. The cloudy sky was threatening but so far had only resulted in streaks of evaporating rain covering the mountain peaks like a veil.

"Seen anything yet?" Laura was at the wheel so David could focus on spotting wildlife, especially grizzlies.

"A squirrel maybe." David squinted at the deep woods outlined by stretches of clearings.

She navigated the section of hilly road about five miles east of Norris Junction to return to their hotel in Cody. They'd had a full day of sightseeing around Yellowstone, including the Old Faithful geyser and Yellowstone Canyon and falls. A mix of their music played, alternative rock for her and heavy metal for him.

Approaching a blind curve, a small red car in front of her suddenly veered into the left lane.

"What the...?" Laura gasped as a prickle of adrenaline shot up her arms.

In a moment, it became clear—a large white pickup loomed in their lane, bearing down on them head on.

She swerved hard left, but too late. The truck smashed into their front passenger side at full speed. With a deafening boom, Laura and David were thrown forward. Their SUV spun 360 degrees as bits of metal shot into the air. The airbags deployed with a punch and then deflated, leaving the acrid odor of explosive charge. Talcum powder drifted through the air like dust motes.

Everything stuttered into slow motion. A geyser of steam erupted from the engine. Laura realized their vehicle was sliding backwards from the force of the collision. She frantically hit the brakes. Nothing. The SUV skidded while the engine hissed. She saw the ravine next to them. With a tremendous jolt, the Nissan slid over a curb and stopped, teetering inches from the edge of the steep drop-off.

Laura turned to David slumped against the passenger window. She shrieked, "David! David!" No response. She had to get out, get help. She desperately pushed at her car door and it refused to budge. They were trapped.

"Help! Help!" Steam poured from the front of the SUV. She scanned the rearview mirror trying to make sense of the chaos in the back. "Puppies, are you hurt?" When the dogs were silent, she was sure they were injured—or worse.

David took a big gulp of air. His chest rose, then stopped. Each few seconds between his irregular breaths seemed to last for minutes.

Panic overtook her. She shoved uselessly on her door, screaming, "He's dying! He's dying!"

Like a mirage, someone peered in her window and tapped on it. "Help us," she pleaded. Men yanked on the driver's side door while Laura pushed. Finally, it rasped open. With another glance at David, she took heart that he was breathing.

A man in a bright green shirt arrived. "I'm a medical doctor." He urged caution as the men helped Laura out of the SUV. They carefully laid her on the ground next to the wreck, supporting her back and neck.

Laura heard someone say, "Possible broken neck." She wasn't sure who they were talking about. Things hazed in an almost hallu-cinogenic way. She wiggled her hands and feet. Other than a deep pain from her seatbelt, she didn't appear to have other major injuries. Whenever she studied the steaming Nissan, a wave of nausea rushed over her. More worrisome, she couldn't see David on the other side of the SUV.

A ranger came up to her and covered her with a blanket.

"We're getting help. Hang in there."

Laura realized she'd been shivering. "What about the dogs? How are our puppies?"

The ranger peered into the back of the vehicle. It sounded to Laura like Jade was furiously barking. "They're fine. We'll take care of them."

"Their leashes are in the back. Make sure they're on them. And they both like wet food."

Two women sat by Laura's side and comforted her until the EMTs arrived. Laura continued to hear barking from the SUV. God, let them both be all right, she prayed. She then remembered the adage to document an accident, and asked one of the women to get the phones from the wreck and take pictures of the scene.

When the woman showed Laura the photos, she gasped. David was splayed on the ground, his leg in an unnatural position. Something else about the scene was odd—then she realized what was different. Their car had spun one hundred eighty degrees from the direction they'd been traveling. The realization of the force of the impact sent a shock wave through her.

An older woman came over, crying. "My son is so sorry. He fell asleep at the wheel. The four of us were tired, and I guess we all nodded off. I thought he was in the best shape to drive."

"Were any of you hurt?" Laura asked.

Shaking her head, she replied in a strong Southern accent, "No, just a little shook up and maybe bruised."

Laura couldn't respond, upset over the obvious injuries David had suffered. She watched the older lady shuffle toward the pickup truck. Veteran park ranger Dave Page arrived shortly after the accident. The compact gray-bearded man knelt next to Laura and patted her hand. "I am so sorry it's taking so long. There were other accidents in the park today. Ambulances for all of you are coming from the Old Faithful area."

Laura held back tears. She knew that was over an hour from them. An hour that David possibly didn't have.

He paused. "Except for...your husband?"

"No. David's a...friend." She didn't know exactly how to describe their new relationship. "What's wrong?"

"He's stable, but we won't wait for an ambulance. He needs to be airlifted to the nearest hospital."

"Oh my God. Where's that?" Laura asked groggily.

"Idaho Falls."

"So far away."

The ranger then asked for contact information, and Laura gave him David's phone with the numbers for his daughter Angie and son Scott.

"And who can I notify for you?"

Laura hesitated. She had no children, and her parents had passed. Her brother was traveling on a cruise with his wife and couldn't be easily reached. The one person who should be her emergency contact wouldn't be able to take a phone call, let alone process the information.

She shook her head. "There's no one."

Minutes dragged like hours, and then she heard the *whup-whup-whup* of the helicopter nearing.

"Thank God, he's getting help," Laura said to the two women with her.

She heard thunder rumbling and the echoes off the surrounding mountains. The sky darkened to a steel gray. A downdraft of cold air blasted from the threatening clouds, sending a chill down her arms followed by a sense of dread.

Then the sound of the helicopter grew fainter.

A ranger spoke into a radio. Kneeling next to her, he said, "The copter can't land in this weather. We're going to ambulance him to the West Yellowstone airstrip and airlift him after the storms pass."

A wave of fear and disappointment washed over Laura. David would lose precious time.

"You'll go by ground and meet him at Idaho Falls Hospital." The first ambulance arrived, red lights strobing across the scene. Her throat tightened as she watched them load David and drive off. Panic overtook her as she realized she might never see him again.

Twenty minutes later, Laura was loaded into a park emergency vehicle as the sky opened up with rain. Once outside Yellowstone, she transferred to a commercial ambulance.

The rangers watched the last of the emergency vehicles drive off, and directed traffic around the crash site. People who'd been patiently sitting in their cars started their engines. The tow trucks arrived and the rangers decided it was time to get the dogs.

"I'll take them home," a woman ranger volunteered.

One of them opened the back hatch and pulled Laila out of her twisted, metal cage. Another ranger reached in and touched Jade's plastic airline carrier. It cracked open like an egg. In a moment, something black and white flashed out the back of the SUV. Like a streak of lightning zigzagging across the open meadow, and despite the calls of the rangers, Jade disappeared into the dark forest.

"How long until we get to Idaho Falls?" Laura asked the EMT. The ambulance hit a bump, shooting stinging pains through her wrist and side. Every tight curve on the mountainous road jarred her ribs as she rocked from side to side.

"It's usually less than two hours, if the weather's good."

Laura checked the clock over the door. They'd left West Yellowstone about forty minutes before.

"Has David's helicopter taken off yet?" His flight had been delayed at the airstrip for the weather that swept through.

The driver answered, "I've had bad cell phone connections. I'll try again."

The EMT next to her frowned. "You sure you don't want anything for the pain? I figure we have about another hour or so."

"No." When she got to David, she wanted to be as alert as possible if he needed her. She tried to keep her breath shallow as any deep inhale sent piercing pains through her chest and ribs. Fear for David rippled through her.

As they neared Idaho Falls, the driver took a phone call. "The helicopter was finally able to land and get David on board. But, they've decided his injuries warrant going to a major trauma center."

"Where's that?" She gasped as she took a deep breath and pain shot through her.

"The helicopter's going to Bozeman."

"*Montana*? Oh my God." The shock that they were going in opposite directions hit her with force. "How...how will I get to him?"

The two paramedics exchanged glances. The driver said, "If we turn around, it'll be another three hours or more."

"I need to be with him. Please."

"And the road's just as bumpy." As if to prove his point, the ambulance hit a rough patch, sending more pain shooting through her.

"Please take me to Bozeman."

Laura knew she had the right to request a hospital.

"Will it jeopardize her condition?" the driver asked. When the other man replied in the negative he added, "Okay we can do it...as long as you understand the additional time."

Nodding, she focused on the clock over the back door, watching every minute tick by. Woozy, she drifted off and woke when the ambulance stopped. The clock read close to nine p.m., a full six hours after the accident.

They rolled Laura's stretcher into the Bozeman Deaconess Hospital emergency room, where she saw David on an exam table. When he grinned at her, she broke into sobs. The EMTs rolled her next to him. Through her tears, she said, "I see they gave us the ER honeymoon suite."

"How are you, darlin'?"

Laura forced a smile. "It's been a pretty long day. How was your first ride in a helicopter?"

He winked. "For the thousands of dollars it must've cost, I didn't even get a window seat."

A doctor walked over to them. "How are you doing, Mr. Sowers?"

"You tell me, Doc."

The young man addressed Laura. "We'll be sending you to radiology soon." He turned to David. "We have your x-ray results." He read off a litany of injuries: fractured wrist, several fingers broken in his right hand, cracked ribs on his right side, concussion. There was also severe bruising. However, David's most serious injury appeared to be his left kneecap, which was shattered in at least ten places. "You'll need an orthopedic surgeon as soon as possible."

Once the doctor left, David asked Laura, "How're our puppies?"

"Fine. The ranger told me they'd keep them for us till we're out of the hospital."

"That's a relief." He closed his eyes.

"Let's try and get some rest." She grabbed David's good hand and held it.

He nodded in agreement and dozed off.

At eleven o'clock that night, Laura fumbled for her cell phone when it rang. As she listened, her mouth turned to cotton batting and then her heart raced. "Which dog? Describe her. Are you sure? It makes no sense."

"What is it? What's wrong?" David asked groggily from the exam table.

She ended the call after listening for a few more seconds. "Jade's missing."

"What do you mean, 'missing'? She was in the back. With Laila."

"Somehow when the rangers went to get her, her carrier fell apart. She ran away from them and wouldn't come back."

"I'm the only one she'll come to." He sat up on the table, and then lay down wincing in pain. "We've got to go get her. *Right now!*"

Chapter Two

"I HAVE TO FIND MY PUP."

TWENTY-FOUR HOURS MISSING—"We can't go tonight. Not a single Bozeman car agency opens until morning." Laura studied her phone. "It'll be a three-hour trip, at least." A wave of relief washed over her; the thought of driving twisting mountainous roads in the dark made her stomach churn. It would be bad enough to get behind the wheel again in daylight. David was in no condition to leave the hospital, let alone drive.

It was after midnight in David's private room where he'd had a recliner put next to his bed for her. Finally, he fell asleep. Occasionally he awakened and grasped her hand. Laura couldn't rest; she worried that David was in no shape to leave the hospital, but eventually decided she'd help him leave if the doctor allowed it.

She also fretted about the accident itself. She had been relatively unhurt, while David was seriously injured and his precious Jade lost in the wilderness. The couple had met only a few months before and were taking a major step by traveling together. They'd even joked that one of them might cut the trip short if they didn't get along and take a Greyhound bus home.

Laura had cajoled David into spending a few days in Yellowstone during a break between her dog agility judging events in Billings, Montana and Jackson, Wyoming. It had been years since he'd taken time away from his small advertising business, Door Hangers Direct, but she finally convinced him it was a great puppy-bonding opportunity.

Besides their love of the outdoors, they had Aussies in common. Early in their relationship, they'd taken Jade and Laila hiking and the dogs acted like littermates. Off-leash they would run ahead at lightning speed, then charge back, nipping playfully at each other.

Jade loved the water, and once at a dog park, she'd jumped into the stream, followed by Laila. When the younger dog realized she was literally in over her head, she'd struggled to the bank with a startled expression that said to Laura, "Why did I do that?" Ever since, Laila had been cautious following the fearless Jade into deep water.

Laura's AKC agility event before the trip to Yellowstone had been held at a fairground horse barn in Billings. She laughed as mares and geldings stuck their heads over the stall doors, watching competing dogs jump the hurdles on the course she'd set up.

Laura told her friend, "The horses are thinking, 'We do that—and a lot better, too!'" In fact, dog agility trials originated as spinoffs of horse jumping competitions in England. In order to be an AKC certified judge, Laura had passed a rigorous two-and-a-half-day test. She was proud of her achievement; on average, only 30 percent of the applicants passed the annual event and usually not on the first try. It was a paid position, and she needed the money.

She worried she would have to cancel two appointments; the next judging event in Cody and her weekly visit to the memory care institution.

As David snored next to her, Laura pondered how much Jade

meant to him. She took heart that his dog had a much better chance of survival than her Laila would've had. Jade was older, faster, stronger, fearless—and had the will of a mule. She could've made a great agility dog, Laura realized, except for her trait of independence. There might be a moment running in a trial when Jade would turn around and walk away, clearly saying the competition was a waste of her time.

By six in the morning, Laura had a taxi take her to the airport, where she picked up a rental car as soon as the doors opened. She returned to Bozeman Deaconess Hospital in time to find David insisting on an early release.

He and Laura wore a combination of Walmart and hospital-issued outfits a kind aide had found for them, replacing the ruined clothing cut off them.

"We resemble that scene in *Pulp Fiction*," Laura noted as they completed the paperwork. "You know, where John Travolta and Samuel L. Jackson are dressed like volleyball players."

"Yeah, you're right." David wore a gray golf shirt emblazoned with *Bozeman Deaconess Hospital*. His oversized athletic shorts, Bronco-colored in navy blue and trimmed in pumpkin orange, hung on his frame like a '90s basketball player. Both of them wore flip-flops, decidedly un-Western wear.

"You've got to get to an orthopedic surgeon, as soon as possible," the doctor cautioned as he studied the papers.

David was emphatic. "I'll go as soon I can."

"Without proper treatment, your shattered knee may never be functional again." He nodded toward David's other bandages. "And you'll want the full use of your hand."

David was a graphic designer, and needed his dominant hand more than most to do his job. "First, I've got to find Jade. I've *got* to find my dog."

The doctor sighed and signed the papers.

A volunteer rolled David out in his wheelchair while Laura drove the rental Ford Flex around to the front of the hospital. Laura scanned the snow-capped mountain peaks ringing Bozeman, and knew she would eventually have to cross mountain ranges during the hundred-mile journey.

The pine-scented air was cool enough to send a chill down her arms. She wondered how cold Jade had been overnight, alone and frightened.

"Big enough?" David asked as he surveyed the crossover SUV. "We could fit seven people in it."

"It's safer than the little compact they tried to give me." She and the young aide helped David stand and then performed an awkward dance to get him into the car with his stiff, braced leg.

"Just as well. I probably wouldn't have fit in a smaller one," David said, trying to find a comfortable position.

Laura had been forewarned by the rental car agency that the most direct road to West Yellowstone was under construction so they had to take the longer route. As she drove the two-lane roads, her heart beat faster and her palms perspired at the approach of every oncoming vehicle. For most of the three-hour drive, the accident replayed again and again in her mind. She tried to hide her fear from David with chitchat.

He stared out the passenger side window, responding with monosyllabic answers to her questions. The road followed the river meandering through a wide valley framed by craggy mountains.

"I bet you'd love to fish here." Laura pointed out a man netting a trout, which sparkled in the sunshine.

"Yeah."

Finally, Laura addressed the real issue. "You're worried we've been gone too long from the scene?"

"That's an understatement." He winced when she hit a bump in the road.

"Sorry about that." Her wrist ached and she struggled to keep a tight hold on the wheel whenever she needed to make a sharp turn.

Laura's phone rang. It was news, either good or bad.

"Can you put it on speaker, David?"

He fumbled with his good hand. Ranger Dave Page said, "I saw Jade this morning near the crash site."

David and Laura looked hopefully at one another. Jade had made it through the night.

"But she ran away again."

They exchanged concerned glances.

"Then around ten this morning, she was spotted by two tourists, but she took off when they called to her."

"Is she okay?" David gnawed at his bottom lip. "I mean did she seem hurt?"

"I don't think so," he assured them. "She ran quickly across the meadow." He then told them where they could pick up Laila, and that he'd meet them near the scene of the accident later.

After they ended the call, Laura smiled at David. "Jade will come to you right away."

"Please go faster."

She knew their chances were better the sooner they could get to the crash site—but the fear that gripped her made her let off the accelerator every time an oncoming car sped toward them.

They stopped at the West ranger station to pick up Laura's dog, who had been cared for overnight by a woman ranger with a warm smile. Laila ran to Laura, ecstatically jumping and barking. As Laura bent down to hug her puppy, she was covered in doggy kisses.

When she saw the metal crate with its bowed wire and several broken joints, her heart sank. She was sure her puppy had been tossed around like a bowling ball, and should be bruised and traumatized from the crash.

"She looks great," Laura admitted, giving her hope for Jade.

The ranger laughed. "She ate well last night, every bit of puppy chow I gave her."

The three of them walked Laila to their rental vehicle. When Laura loaded the crate into the back and opened the rear door, Laila jumped in without hesitation. The Aussie acted unfazed. Maybe Jade too had recovered from any trauma.

"We'd better get going." David eyed the long line of vehicles inching into the entrance to the park.

"We get over four million visitors a year." The ranger frowned. "And most of them come during the summer, of course." When David groaned, she told them she had an idea. "Follow me in your car."

She hopped on a bike and led them down a gravel road to a back access to the park, therefore bypassing the traffic tie-up. After she unlocked the gate, she waved them through. They thanked her profusely; she'd taken care of Laila and probably saved them over an hour of frustrating wait time.

The heavy late July tourist traffic was atrocious. At a traffic jam, they found the tourists gawking at a bison. They were stymied by another tie-up only a few minutes later.

"It's just another freakin' buffalo." David muttered.

"Get over it, people." Laura added. "It's not a bear-jam."

A park ranger's vehicle was stopped next to the herd, a loud *thud-thud-thud* coming from a speaker.

"What the heck is that noise?" David craned his head around the parked cars.

"I guess it's to get them to move."

Bison swung their heads toward the vehicle with an expression that read, "Bring it on." Eventually, the huge beasts inched their way off the road.

Exasperated and frazzled, the couple arrived at the accident site mid-afternoon. The journey, which should've lasted three hours, had taken five. The scene had been cleared of all traces of the collision.

Ranger Page waited for them as they turned into the nearest turnout to where Jade had been lost. He walked over to their rental car and after greeting them, nodded toward Laila in her crate.

"Right after Jade ran out, we put your other dog on leash trying to lure her back."

"That's a good thought." David knew neither of them was healthy enough to walk a headstrong puppy today. "Maybe we'll leave her with the windows down and Jade will hear her."

"Good idea," Laura agreed. "She certainly barks a lot." Laila answered with a few yips from the back seat.

"And we thought this might help." Ranger Page pointed to an animal-print comforter on the ground. "We left it here, hoping the scent would draw your dog."

David nodded, his voice breaking. "Her crate pad. She was never without it." It had been very thoughtful of the rangers to grab it from the wrecked SUV.

"And he's on lookout." The ranger nodded toward a bored-looking young man at the edge of the woods. "Recently, she was spotted between Ice Lake and Wolf Lake. It's about three miles from here."

"Thanks." Laura nodded toward the forest. "Are there bears or wolves nearby?"

He shrugged. "Not that I know of, but there's wildlife everywhere. At least the coyotes have been cleared out of this area by the wolves."

David found this anything but encouraging. He screwed up his courage and asked, "How long has a dog...." He forced the words out. "Survived in Yellowstone?"

"As far as I know," Ranger Page hesitated. "About two weeks."

David didn't answer, but scanned the meadow.

Ranger Page checked his watch. "We'll come back around sunset and see how you're doing."

David grinned. "We'll call you when we get her and save you the trip."

They thanked the ranger and watched as he drove away. "Jade should come any second now," David told Laura. Unable to walk, he sat in the car near the epicenter of the crash.

"Yep. Here puppy, puppy." Laura walked around the area with

aching knees, which had slammed against the dashboard in the collision.

David started to whistle for Jade then stopped, looking ruefully at his broken right fingers. He lifted his left hand instead. "Check out the woods. She's around here somewhere."

Laura peered into the dark pine forest. "I think I see something… black and white…." Then dejectedly, she realized it was only dappled sunlight and shadows.

They decided to drive to the Ice Lake Trailhead after half an hour of searching. At the parking area, Laura got out of the car. She locked her gaze with David's. She knew he could barely walk, let alone hike. "I'll go look for her."

"Are you sure?" When she nodded, he said, "Then make lots of noise, and don't spend an extra minute."

She walked down the road to the trailhead festooned in warning signs.

BEAR ATTACK – CAN YOU AVOID ONE?

MAKE NOISE

No problem there. She planned to call like crazy for Jade.

CARRY BEAR SPRAY

Laura gulped. She didn't have any of the super-strong pepper spray on her, let alone "bear bells," commonly used to make additional noise to let bears know you were human.

AVOID HIKING ALONE

She glanced around at the quiet, empty woods. Maybe she'd meet some hikers along the way…human hikers.

DO NOT RUN

Wearing flip-flops rather than her usual hiking boots, she realized she'd never be able to sprint very fast. Anyway, she knew she could never outrun a bear. She remembered scientists had clocked grizzlies at Yellowstone going 30 miles an hour for a couple of miles. And they were loping, not even breaking a sweat. A shiver ran through her. At least she knew what she was up against. Jade was quick, but was she fast enough?

The sign went on to offer more detailed advice. Surprise encounter? Slowly back away. If bear attacks? Stand your ground and use your bear spray, the sign advised. Well, that wasn't an option, she thought as she set out down the trail. She'd have to employ the last ditch strategy—play dead.

Even in flip-flops, she found the empty trail an easy walk. She was acutely aware of every rustle in the dense forest. She passed fallen trees strewn like pickup sticks, charred in the 1988 wildfires that burned over a third of Yellowstone's forests. Heart pounding, every ten feet or so she called out, "Here Jade, here puppy, puppy." She fervently hoped she would attract the dog—and not a wolf or grizzly.

Then Laura spotted movement in the dark forest. She froze. "Here…puppy…puppy." Her voice came out as a squeak. She held her breath as some scrub bushes moved. Something *was* moving. "Puppy?" A golden-mantled ground squirrel scurried up a spruce, a pinecone in its mouth. Laura let out a deep breath.

After about half an hour, she arrived at Ice Lake, a pristine sparkling body of water ringed in tall lodgepole pines. Perched on the shore, an orange round tent marked a campground. Laura waved at the two young women sitting by the shoreline.

Walking up to them, she asked, "Have you seen a black and white dog? She's an Australian shepherd, commonly mistaken for a Border collie."

"No, sorry," one of them replied. "How did you lose her?"

When Laura explained, they immediately expressed their sympathy and promised to keep an eye out for Jade.

"Just call the rangers if you spot her."

"Good luck," they called out after Laura.

She was beginning to realize how much she was going to need it.

Laura rejoined David and they drove back to the accident site. David sat on Jade's blanket. Their failure showed on their long faces. "Could you hear me calling her when I was on the trail?" Laura asked.

"Only for a little while. Could you hear me?"

"I thought I heard you whistle a couple of times when I first set out."

"So sound isn't traveling very far." He snorted. "We only have over two million acres to cover."

"But she's been spotted recently." She patted his good hand and smiled.

"You're right. Hold out hope."

David had trained Jade from the time she was a small pup to stay out of the road. Even so, flashes of fear cut through them as a continual stream of vehicles zipped by only yards away as they searched the high mountain meadow.

"She's very cautious around traffic," Laura offered to console David.

"Yeah." His frown told her he was still worried that Jade, disoriented and frightened, might dart across the road.

After calling for another half an hour, David asked in a hoarse voice, "Do you think she's anywhere near here?"

"Maybe she is, but she might be scared..." and possibly injured, she added silently to herself. The rangers' hats and David's baseball cap gave her an idea.

The first two nights of this trip, they'd stayed at the Red Lodge KOA campground. Sitting on the rustic porch with their two dogs, Jade had begun a frenzy of barking at an elderly man using a cane and wearing a hat. "What if she's afraid of people in hats? Even us?"

"It's worth a try." He tossed his aside as they called out again.

An older man and woman drove up to them. "Are you the people who lost your dog?"

When David nodded enthusiastically, the couple continued. "The rangers told us you were here. We saw a black and white dog coming up to stopped cars nearby, but as soon as they opened their doors, the dog bolted from them."

"She's still around here, then." David scanned the meadow.

Fueled by adrenaline, they got in the car and widened their search to the Virginia Cascade gravel road and the nearby stream. Jade had always loved water, so they drove the one-way, two-and-a-half-mile road, calling out the windows. David whistled for her, using his good left hand. Laila barked from the back, adding her own pleas.

Once they spotted a flash of red fur along the road as they headed back to the meadow. A sliver of hope rose in Laura. "If a fox could make it here, maybe Jade will be okay."

"Maybe. She's as sly as one."

Mountain peaks tinged golden as they and the rangers arrived back at the turnout near the accident site. Ranger Page looked sympathetically at them. "Any sign of your dog?"

"No." David stared at the edge of the woods.

"We can stop traffic for about fifteen minutes. Then I have to let them through." He hypothesized Jade was possibly frightened by the sounds of vehicles. "We can do it a couple of times."

Hope rose in Laura. "It's worth a try."

Relieved that the constant flow of cars had ceased, the couple continued to call and whistle. After the traffic noise stopped, an eerie silence enveloped them after every call, emphasizing how lonely Jade must be. Occasionally, Laila's barks joined in.

At eight thousand feet, the air was already chilly. Goosebumps ran down Laura's arms and she thought of Jade alone at night. "I'd better walk Laila." Laura managed to leash her, but the puppy was so excited to be out of the car, she pulled hard. "*Ouch.*" Pain shot through Laura's ribs and wrist. A ranger noticed and walked over.

"Let me help." He took Laila's leash in hand. "These Aussie's are full of energy, aren't they?"

"That's very kind of you." She watched him walk her dog at a trot. Australian shepherds needed their exercise. Without physical and mental stimulation, Laura knew they could turn their boredom and excess energy into destructive behaviors like chewing their owners' possessions to shreds.

She crossed her fingers, hoping the natural agility, speed, and intelligence that Jade had been bred for would serve her well in the wilderness if they didn't find her tonight.

Ranger Dave walked over to David. "I'm afraid I'm going to have to call it a day. You should too."

David scanned the darkening woods. The predators would soon be active. "Just a few more minutes. I'm sure she's nearby."

"Okay. But we're going to have to let traffic through."

David turned to Laura. "We'd better try and find a place to stay in Yellowstone. It's a long ride to the motel in Cody."

Laura made frantic phone calls, explaining they were the people who had lost their dog. The reservationist found them a room at the Canyon Lodge, across from the Visitor's Center.

A half hour later, David studied the lengthening shadows. "I can't stand the thought of Jade out here another night."

"I know." Two nights, she thought. At least Jade had survived one. "She was spotted today. That should give us hope."

"I'm tryin' to keep that in mind."

With every unanswered call, their optimism faded with the knowledge their beloved puppy was not about to appear from behind a tree. Finally, exhausted and aching, they sat on Jade's blanket. David ran his hand over the soft surface, as if he were petting his dog.

"Jade...Jade." Their calls and whistles echoed off the craggy mountains.

Chapter Three

JADE'S EMPTY BOWL

TWO DAYS MISSING—Laura watched a steady stream of vehicles move along the road. She imagined annoyed campers on their way to their campground, tourists in a hurry to find dinner, or people returning to their hotel after a day of sightseeing. Few of them slowed as they drove by the rental car and the man sitting on the ground, his braced leg out in front of him. Laura paced the area calling for Jade, while Laila slept in her crate.

"It's time to go, David. It's getting too dark to see."

He nodded and struggled into the SUV. Laura then drove to Canyon Village, about eight miles toward the east. Whenever another vehicle approached, her heart thudded. Entering the town, she spotted the familiar modern lodge-like structure, the Canyon Visitor Education Center, which had closed for the day. Adjacent, the Yellowstone General Store glowed brightly in the growing darkness, advertising food and souvenirs. Across the street was the service station. Behind the gas pumps, several cars and trucks were stored in a back lot.

David's wrecked SUV had been towed there after the accident. They exited their rental car and limped toward the wrecks.

Laura stopped short at a white Dodge pickup truck glistening under the overhead lights. The front end was smashed on the passenger side, twisting the enormous chrome grill into a sneer.

Her palms were sweaty, and her heart pounded. "That's the one."

David shook his head. "I didn't even see it coming."

They turned to their own black SUV and gasped. The vehicle was crushed like a soda can. David put his good arm around her. "We're all lucky to be alive."

The windshield was a spiderweb of broken glass, the front hood folded in half.

Tearfully, Laura agreed. But, she thought, Jade is lost.

David's wrecked Nissan was worse than they remembered. Broken glass like green jewels littered the interior, and rain had poured in the open windows, soaking the upholstery and their belongings. They wrenched on the doors, to no avail.

The cooler where they'd stored the makings of a picnic was smashed—a broken wine bottle, cheese, and decaying apples littered the floor. The back seat had collapsed. Laura fought a wave of nausea for the dogs: the terrific jolt as they hit the other vehicle, the spinning and skidding across the pavement, and the final sickening lurch to a stop.

As Laura and David stood in front of the car, they noticed the people pumping gas staring at them. Others cast them quizzical glances as they left the service station. An older couple walked over and asked if they had been in the wreck, eyeing David's sling and leg brace.

"I can't believe you survived this," exclaimed the woman.

David agreed. "But I lost my dog, Jade."

"Here? In Yellowstone?" The older woman started to say something, then bit her lip. "I'm so sorry."

They tried to find something to salvage. Laura's sunglasses were on the floor of the SUV, broken and shattered. She rubbed her empty finger. Somehow, she'd lost a ring she'd been wearing at the time of the accident, but it was nowhere to be found.

"There's really nothing to save." David leaned shakily on the vehicle.

"I'm not hungry but we need to eat." Laura rubbed the goosebumps on her arm. The night was quickly cooling. "And a few more layers wouldn't hurt."

She drove to the Yellowstone General Store and left David in the car. The sprawling mid-century building overflowed with every souvenir imaginable: mugs, glasses, books, and clothing. Center stage stood an enormous stuffed toy moose. She smiled ironically. She'd been hoping to spot a moose in Yellowstone.

Standing in front of stacks and piles of clothing, she numbly wondered what to buy, then grabbed a warmer outfit for each of them. Everything had *Yellowstone* emblazoned on it. Sure, she thought, most people would want to remember their trip. Then she went to the food bar and picked up two cheeseburgers, fries, and sodas.

As Laura checked out, the friendly attendant smiled and asked, "How's your vacation going? Are you having a good time?"

She choked back tears. "We were in the crash yesterday, the ones who lost their dog."

The woman's face softened with sympathy. "We all heard about that. I am so sorry." She pressed a few keys on the register. "The food and drinks are on the house."

"Thank you." She described Jade and where she was last seen.

"I'll let my coworkers know."

A tiny hope sprouted in her. Maybe the more people who knew about Jade's plight, the more likely she'd be spotted soon.

In the Canyon Lodge cabin, Laura and David sat at a rustic log table. The queen-sized beds matched the western motif, and under most circumstances, Laura would describe the room as cozy.

Tonight, all she could focus on was Laila stretched out on the blue carpet and the void where Jade should be.

David picked up a fry. "I keep wondering what Jade is eating." His dog had an internal clock that went off at every mealtime and she would stare him down until fed her usual puppy chow. "The fussy little girl. She only eats wet food and leaves half of it behind."

Laura put some ketchup on her burger, took a bite, and set it down. She could barely swallow, and knew Laila would get her sandwich.

"Why isn't she coming to us?" David put his head in his hands. His burger was untouched.

"I don't know. She must be traumatized." Laura regarded her dog. She thought Laila was too young to make it alone in Yellowstone and knew that Jade had a better chance of survival. But David's attachment to Jade was deep, and her loss would leave a empty space in his heart. Neither of them had imagined the airline carrier would break in a crash. The prospect of disaster hadn't occurred to them.

An uneasy silence surrounded them as David fed Laila his burger.

That night, as they lay in bed fitful with pain, David knew he had to go home the next day. His small business needed him. He'd taken a chance and started his advertising company in 2004. It had been tough; when he'd reluctantly left for the trip to Yellowstone, he had just begun to recover from the Great Recession of 2008.

Even more urgently, he had to get to an orthopedic surgeon. While his broken bones were in casts and his shattered kneecap braced, he had been warned at the hospital he should get further attention as soon as possible to avoid permanent disfigurement. He desperately needed a functioning right hand for his business as a graphic artist and designer. Laura had been able to get him an appointment the upcoming Monday. It would take them most of the day to drive to Cody to pick up their belongings at the motel and return home.

"I have to go." He wiped a tear from his eye. "I don't want to leave Jade, but I have to."

There was nothing Laura could add.

The next morning, they returned to the scene of the accident. David sat in the car calling for Jade. Laura walked the general area with her dog. Laila enjoyed the stroll, and only occasionally sniffed the ground. After consulting her phone, Laura realized she'd spent over two hours searching. They had a long drive home, and she returned to David, hoping for the best. When she saw his face, she knew there wasn't good news.

"Jade's not coming, is she?" David scanned the woods. "I thought...." Tears ran down his cheeks, and he swiped them off. Pain and worry etched lines on his face.

"We should go." Laura pointed at Jade's crate blanket. "What do you want to do about that?"

"Leave it. Who knows? Maybe she'll smell it and come back." He added since Jade was microchipped, if anyone were to catch her, they might take her to a vet or shelter to check her identity.

The two-lane road to Casper passed through mountain scenery. Several times, Laura panicked if an oncoming pickup truck neared the centerline as she relived the crash. David didn't appear to notice Laura's fright, absorbed in his own physical and emotional pain. They barely spoke on the long drive. No matter what they said, one or both of them started crying. All either of them could think of was how frightened Jade must be.

Laila rode in the back in her bent crate. She had jumped right in to it. However, she was quiet throughout the ride and Laura assumed her dog was bruised and sore. She admired her resilient Aussie. She mentally crossed her fingers that Jade was doing as well.

"I can't believe we're leaving my pup up there," David said after several hours of silence.

"We have no choice. You have to get to the doctor. And surgeon."

"I'm never going to see Jade again. I'll just have to accept that fact." He broke down.

This time, Laura didn't argue. She knew the odds had rapidly dropped when they hadn't found Jade right away.

After a twelve-hour drive, they arrived late at Laura's two-story house in a cul-de-sac. An ancient Toyota Sienna van—her dog van—was parked in the driveway in front of her three-car garage. On its rear bumper a sticker read *I'd rather be bar hopping*, with a drawing of an Aussie jumping a hurdle. The other boasted *My Australian shepherd is smarter than your honor student* above a Colorado license plate JMP4FUN.

Laura helped David navigate around the dog agility equipment in her living room, and settled him on the couch. Laura's other two dogs ran joyously to greet her. They had been cared for by a neighbor while she'd been in Yellowstone. Her male Aussie, Karros, was Laura's current agility dog. He was a blue merle with a distinctive coat with patches of white, tan, black, and gray. His show name was "Who's on First."

Eight-and-a-half-year-old Wiki, a Golden Retriever, was the old lady of the pack. Laura had unsuccessfully run her in agility trials. The dog was on the large side, and slow to turn, so much so that Laura compared her Golden to a "semitruck" and her Aussie to a "Ferrari." Additionally, Wiki wasn't competitive with her friendly Golden personality. She would get in the ring, act as if the judge was her friend, and take a detour to say "hi." Her attitude was, "Look! The sun is shining and it's a beautiful day! What is all this running and jumping about?"

Only a few months before, Laura had acquired Laila, a tri-colored puppy. With a show name of "She's a Knockout," Laura informally christened her after Muhammad Ali's champion boxing daughter, Laila. Still too young to train for the rigors of agility, Laura had plans to work with the young Aussie when she was around two years of age and fully grown.

Laura settled David on the couch surrounded by pillows, where he promptly fell asleep. She sat on the floor beside him while the dogs nuzzled her and licked away the tears streaming down her face.

The next morning, after another pain-filled night's sleep, Laura drove David to his house a few miles from her home.

"Scott's here," David said, noting his son's car parked by the detached garage. Scott had driven the four hours from Crested Butte, Colorado, where he worked marketing the ski resort.

Although David shared custody of his children with his ex-wife, over the years they'd spent much of their time with him enjoying many of his interests. Twenty-four-year-old Angie lived with David, having recently graduated from cosmetology school.

Laura helped David into the front door, where Angie and Scott rushed toward him. The anguish was clear on their faces as they peppered him with questions about the accident, the hospital, and Jade.

They helped make David as comfortable as possible on his beige corduroy sofa, propping up his leg and arm with pillows. David's thriving plants lined the light oak hardwood floors. Family photographs covered the walls. A portrait of David holding a two-year-old Scott hung directly across from them.

"We're so glad you're alive." Angie held her dad's hand. "But what happened to Jade?"

David recounted the story as best he could.

Angie frowned. "I'm so confused. First, I got a call from a woman ranger the night of the accident. She told me you were hurt but going to be okay. She said, 'Your dog is fine, she's with me'."

"That's because she had Laila. I called you and told you Jade had got away..."

"I thought the ranger lost her...."

Scott scratched his head. "I still don't get it."

Laura said her goodbyes and walked away from the conversation. On her way out, she spotted some things on the kitchen floor. Quietly, she emptied the water bowl, grabbed the bag of Purina puppy chow, and picked up scattered toys.

One in particular, a plush foot-long yellow bird—Tweety—gave her pause. It was Jade's favorite toy, one of the few the dog hadn't been able to destroy.

Carrying the pile to the garage, she stowed it in a cabinet, hoping to save David a constant reminder of his lost dog. Not that he wouldn't be thinking of his pup day and night anyway, she realized as she let herself out. It would be impossible for either of them not to imagine Jade alone in the wilderness of Yellowstone.

Jade was David's third Australian shepherd. He'd owned a part-Aussie, part-Cattle dog in the '90s named Shadow, and although he'd had dogs all of his life, she was the best. She was smart, loyal, and friendly. He'd been hooked on Aussies ever since. After his ex-wife got Shadow in the divorce decree, his kids brought home another Aussie for him. David promptly named him Ozzy and they were buddies for ten years. David was devastated when he lost Ozzy to cancer in 2012. After that, he put much of his energy and time into his small business, but missed his hiking friend.

Angie and Scott knew how much the dog had meant to him, a constant companion at home and work every day. Two years later, they cajoled him into selecting an Aussie for a Father's Day present. Angie called Bonato Aussies, a breeder who had two litters, one group about four weeks old and a single bi-color left from a previous one.

They liked the breeder, who stated on his website:

We breed for an Australian shepherd that is sound in mind and body with outstanding health, temperament, and intelligence. All our puppies are handled daily, so they are very socialized by the time they go to their new homes. None of our dogs, including our puppies, are kept in kennels except at night. They are all raised in an open environment as part of our family, which we feel is a very important part of their socialization process.

Angie and David watched the tumbling puppies frolicking in the open area. One of them grabbed a small twig and ran circles around the others. Several of its siblings chased it, attempting to take the branch away. The pups drank from a pan of water and busied themselves digging in the dirt below it. Chasing each other and rolling over on the ground, the Aussies were the epitome of happy dogs.

They studied all of the puppies, but Angie immediately felt sorry for a slightly larger black and white pup, who sat behind the rest of the blue merle Aussies. The breeder had told them the female was the last one from a prior litter.

"What about this one, Dad?" She held up the squirming black and white Aussie with bright blue eyes. "Look, she even has a Marilyn Monroe beauty mark." She pointed to the round brown spot on her white muzzle.

"She does resemble a movie star. Maybe with the attitude to go with it."

The puppy stopped squirming and gazed directly at him. David nodded toward the marbled black, white, and gray puppy attacking one of its siblings. "What about this blue merle?"

"I still like this one." Angie held the puppy and stared into the soulful gaze. If they didn't take her home, the pup would be at the breeders for a long time, as people would likely pick the younger ones. "She has the most beautiful eyes."

David regarded the intelligent stare of light blue gemstones. A chill ran through him and he wondered if the black and white dog could read his mind. She was a little over eight weeks of age, and he swore this dog managed to have a dignity some dogs never achieved.

"She needs us," Angie added. "Nobody's taken her."

David petted the older puppy, and she licked his hand. "Okay. You win." It hadn't been a tough sell for him. She was gorgeous and had a spirited quality about her he couldn't quite label.

As soon as Angie set the little Aussie down, she looked up at David and smiled.

"I guess she's happy about it, Dad."

The snuggling pup rode the whole way home in Angie's lap, as if understanding she'd joined a loving family.

"I think we should name her 'Jade,' for her blue eyes."

"Isn't jade green?"

"There's a blue shade that supposedly attracts peace and serenity." The puppy wiggled in Angie's lap.

David wasn't sure if the active puppy would attract anything other than chaos, but he had already fallen hard, finding Jade's hypnotic stare and wide smile irresistible.

As time went on, he realized Jade had the independence, intelligence—and stubbornness—of her breed. On a three-mile hike, then six-month-old Jade ran ahead on the trail toward the parking lot. After she disappeared around a corner, David jogged down to the trailhead calling her name. No Jade. Upset and fearful, he decided to return to his car to grab some treats to lure her. He reached the trailhead where at least thirty other vehicles were parked. As he opened the SUV, Jade emerged from beneath it, wiggling with pleasure to see him. Relieved, he figured she knew their car by scent.

David reminded his children of Jade's escapades while they strategized what to do about their missing puppy.

"Our dog has a mind of her own," Angie admitted. "Just the other day she refused to leave the car after we got home."

David often had trouble getting her to come to him when he called her. "She's independent all right."

"And what will she eat?" Scott asked, taking a bite of pizza.

David worried more about what might eat *her.* Weakened by the cold and lack of food, Jade could make an easy target for wolves and coyotes. He hoped somehow her resourcefulness would keep her safe until she was found.

Angie exchanged a look with her brother. "Scott and I made a decision. We're going to Yellowstone next week to find her."

Scott added, "I'd already arranged some time off for my birthday. Perfect time to go."

David drew in a sharp breath. "It'll be expensive...."

"Naw. We'll tent-camp." Scott was a true Coloradoan who loved the outdoors in all forms, just like his father.

Angie glanced anxiously at her brother. "Or sleep in our cars."

A sense of dread enveloped David. Normally, he would encourage any effort by his kids to find his beloved Jade. But things had gone so wrong since that fateful afternoon in Yellowstone where his world had changed forever. Fear and concern shot through him. In his emotional state, try as he might, he just couldn't imagine a good outcome.

Chapter Four

LAURA'S STORY

THREE DAYS MISSING—Laura drove home from David's house with aching ribs, her wrist throbbing with every turn of the steering wheel. She dreaded her upcoming chore, more painful and sad than her injuries. She had to contact the memory care institution for her weekly update on her husband, Quinn.

He had been diagnosed six long years before, and confined for almost three. It was difficult to visit as every time she saw him his condition had deteriorated, breaking her heart anew.

They'd met in 1986, both working for the same office supply company at different locations. Quinn would stop by, and while Laura filed invoices, she would glance at the tall, handsome man who had reminded her of Richard Gere.

"You two should go out sometime," her coworker suggested. "You have a lot in common."

"If he ever notices me." Laura watched him making small talk with her manager. He strode away without apparently registering her existence. After asking around, she learned she and Quinn lived on opposite sides of Denver's Washington Park—called "Wash Park" by locals—one of the oldest and most historic neighborhoods. Laura rented a room in a friend's small bungalow near the park. It was comfortable, even with its tiny bedrooms, old kitchen, and an octopus of a furnace in the basement.

On one early summer afternoon, it was a perfect day to walk her Golden Retriever, Bear. They strolled tree-lined streets beneath a royal blue Colorado sky, past cozy Craftsman homes with their sturdy pillars and open porches decorated with hanging fuchsia and ferns. She inhaled the sweet aroma of early roses wafting from the well-tended gardens.

As a car slowed for a stop sign ahead of her, she heard music from the open window and recognized the driver. Her heart sped up and Bear pulled on the leash, lunging toward the vehicle.

"Hi, Quinn." Laura was pulled to the car where Bear placed her paws on the door and stuck her head in the open window. Quinn vigorously petted and fussed over the Golden, who was in rapture as he rubbed her ears. They had dogs in common, she thought, but, hello, what about me?

"You know we both work at Pencils?"

He smiled. "You're not an intern?"

"No." Was he dense or what?

"Well then, I'll see you around."

She pulled Bear toward her and he drove off.

"That went well. At least for you, Bear."

As it happened, Quinn *had* noticed her. He asked her out shortly afterward to a Nuggets' basketball game. On that first date, Laura proceeded to spill her huge Coke, which cascaded down the stairs. Quinn jumped up and ran to get napkins to stem the flow.

"Sorry, sorry." Laura inwardly cursed her nervousness. "I don't know what happened."

"No problem." As he wiped up the sticky mess, he continued to smile at her. Her stomach flipped, this time definitely not from nerves.

On their second date, when Quinn picked her up to go golfing, he eyed Laura's very professional-looking golf clubs as he carried them to his car.

"Blades, aren't they?"

"Yeah, my dad bought them for me." Laura noticed it was his turn to be nervous.

On his first swing, Quinn hit the ball hard—right into a tree. It didn't get better for him the entire game. Laura tried to hide her smile as his golf balls bounced and ricocheted off almost every hazard.

That night, she recounted her date to her mom on the phone.

"Honey," her mother chided, "if you keep beating men at golf you'll never get a husband."

They were married in 1989 in a small ceremony with close friends and family. Bear was in attendance, and they joked that the Golden Retriever had picked Quinn for Laura.

They both had successful careers in sales, and when children didn't come, built a close relationship filled with shared interests in golf, hiking, skiing, travel, and dogs. They developed their own intimate traditions. They started and ended every day with a kiss. If they missed their morning ritual, Quinn would drive over to Laura's workplace and plant a large kiss on her to the approving smiles of her coworkers.

Laura became interested in AKC dog agility events in the summer of 2002. At first, she enjoyed watching, but soon started training her Golden, Kalani. She was Laura's "heart dog," that once in a lifetime—maybe twice if she would be truly blessed—soul mate dog. They had an understanding, a bond stronger than most, and a special level of communication.

Kalani would jump through fire for Laura and won the novice title in 2004. Most importantly, Laura had found a community of like-minded people. All of them were dog-lovers and enjoyed friendly competition. Soon, she had a large circle of friends.

Quinn attended the shows with Laura, cheering her on. He decorated their fourth bedroom and dedicated it to their Golden Retrievers. He painted the walls to match their coats and put up her ever-growing collection of ribbons and pictures of their dogs with their titles.

She would need to cling to the memories of good times when the future took a decided turn.

Quinn forgot Laura's birthday in 2007. He'd always been thoughtful, buying her cards, flowers, and presents for all special occasions. She wrote it off to stress; they were both busy with work.

Then, early in 2009, Quinn's driving became erratic. He would pull out in front of cars, setting off a round of honking and rude gestures.

"Didn't you see that truck?" Laura's heart thumped.

"Of course I did. The guy was going too fast."

It appeared different to her, but she kept her mouth shut when she saw the rage on Quinn's face.

Other times, he would be in the wrong lane to turn, and get furious when people wouldn't let him in. He'd stop his car, hitting the horn until he eventually made his way across the highway, sometimes running over the curb. Laura feared it was just a matter of time before he might have a serious accident.

Managing eight salespeople in a territory covering every state west of the Mississippi, Laura traveled extensively. Quinn couldn't remember where she'd been. Sometimes she would come home late at night to a locked garage, and had to pound on the door to get the dogs to awaken Quinn. Furious, she wondered if she was no longer important to him, and their relationship was ending after twenty years of happy marriage.

When Quinn forgot her birthday again, she was hurt and frightened, fearing he had fallen out of love with her. Or perhaps he'd been drinking too much. She traveled so often that it wasn't possible to keep tabs on him.

"It's just not like you."

"I'm having some memory issues, that's all." He laughed. "I even left my laptop at work the other day. Just plain old forgot to get it." He kissed her, apologizing for his lapse.

Reassured he still loved her, she started to worry about his memory and personality changes. In November 2009, she left her job that required so much travel. She planned to take a few months off to unwind—and to keep an eye on Quinn.

In February 2010, Quinn and Laura took a trip to Scottsdale, Arizona for an agility show with their three dogs, including a Golden, Wiki, Quinn's heart dog. Laura convinced him to let her do most of the driving. They stayed at a Marriot a mile away from the WestWorld event center where the trials were held. After a day of golfing with other husbands, Quinn returned to pick up Laura. She wanted to stay a little longer to watch the rest of the competition.

She asked friends, John and Betty, if they wouldn't mind taking Quinn back to the hotel.

The next day, Betty asked Laura, "Did Quinn tell you about our experience yesterday driving him?"

"No...should he have?" Unease crept through Laura, raising the hair on her arms.

Betty regarded her intently. "It turned out to be quite the excursion. We had to drive around for an hour trying to find the hotel. All Quinn could remember was that it was near a golf course and an airport. Of course, it was only about a mile from here." She frowned. "I found it surprising he couldn't even recall it was a Marriot."

Laura knew then something was seriously wrong. She fought a rising panic and immediately found a job with less travel.

That September, Quinn's coworker, Costen, and his wife, Paula, a registered nurse, invited Laura and Quinn for dinner. Laura drove over from an agility trial and met Quinn there. After greeting them,

Laura said, "I'd better walk the dogs." She'd left them in the car.

"I'll join you," Paula volunteered.

"Sure." Laura was puzzled at how eager the nurse was to walk with her.

After a few minutes Paula asked, "Did you know Quinn lost his job last week?"

Laura stopped short. "I...I...no. I didn't."

Paula's face softened in sympathy. "He was having memory issues at work, making mistakes, and getting angry at people."

"I knew he was having sales problems." Her stomach knotted. "I didn't know about the rest."

"You should get him checked right away." Paula stopped and stared at Laura. "His symptoms are consistent with a brain tumor." She hesitated. "Or Alzheimer's."

"It can't be. He's too young. He's only in his fifties." One of the dogs leaned against her leg.

Paula shook her head. "It's rare, but possible. People in their thirties can exhibit symptoms."

"At least it may not be cancer."

"No...but Alzheimer's would be worse."

She'd thought it was Quinn's drinking. Now she wasn't certain.

Quinn was sitting on the couch, watching television. Laura walked in front of him, blocking his view of the Bronco game.

"When were you going to tell me you lost your job?" She struggled to control her anger.

"I...I was going to tell you tonight."

Laura seriously doubted it.

She made an appointment with their family doctor the next day. In the waiting room, Quinn nonchalantly leafed through the old magazines. Laura's stomach twisted with anxiety. Once in the examination room, Laura told the doctor everything that had happened: losing his job, memory lapses, anger, his total change in personality. Quinn sat passively by, as if detached from the whole discussion.

The doctor listened. She immediately prescribed anti-depressants for Quinn and scheduled him for a sleep apnea test, MRI, and other tests to rule out a brain tumor, alcoholism, and depression. They left the office with Laura in a daze.

Waiting for the test results at home, Laura frantically researched the symptoms Quinn displayed. Please don't let it be Alzheimer's, she chanted to herself, wiping tears from her eyes. There was no cure, no way to stop the relentless progression of the deadly disease.

She dared to study photographs of Quinn over the past few years. She admitted to herself she could see the vacant expression on his face increasing with time. In the latest pictures in Scottsdale, he stared blankly into the distance and she hardly recognized the man she'd been married to for over twenty years.

A week later, the doctor's office called. In the examination room, Laura's heart pounded while Quinn sat calmly. Laura noticed his expressionless face.

When the doctor entered, she said, "The MRI results show some small gray spots."

"What does that mean?" Laura glanced anxiously at Quinn, as her mind raced to recall if that signaled any particular disease.

The doctor appeared uneasy. "It can mean a number of things. Let's try a test here, Quinn." She explained it consisted of thirty questions and was a standard test for long- and short-term memory ability.

Quinn could only remember a single word in each of the questions—at best. Laura knew he was frustrated as he laughed and coughed to give himself more time to try to remember. The doctor said some words, but only a few registered. "Probably early-onset Alzheimer's."

Laura's mind raced, trying to recount the facts she'd found on the internet. The vast majority of Alzheimer's patients were over 65.

"Are you sure?"

"I'll refer you to a neurologist, but I'm fairly certain." She handed Laura the doctor's name.

Quinn paled. He seemed to register the probable diagnosis.

Laura sat stunned. This is it, she thought. Our lives will be changed forever. In her heart, she knew the doctor was probably right. She'd been in denial.

"How am I going to handle this? How do I take care of him?"

She shrugged. "You'll need to put locks on the house so he doesn't wander off."

Furious with the doctor's cavalier answer, Laura led Quinn into the parking lot. Before the diagnosis, she'd been so frustrated with him. Now, she guiltily realized it wasn't his fault and he couldn't control his behavior.

As if reading her mind Quinn said, "You could leave me if it's Alzheimer's."

She reached for his hand as she saw a glimmer of her best friend, her lover, the man she'd been married to for over twenty years. "Of course not." But her heart ached for what the future would bring.

Shortly afterward, the neurologist confirmed advanced stage early-onset Alzheimer's.

Laura reacted to the diagnosis by deciding to take life one day at a time, and enjoy what time they had left together. She reminded Quinn daily of what a great life they'd had up to this point. He still loved golf and they would play most weekends. Eventually, he couldn't remember the number of his golf strokes nor was he able to add up the scorecard. His game worsened as his motor skills declined. He became frustrated and angry on the course, and Laura's heart broke at seeing him lose something he had loved.

They went to many movies as his memory declined. He couldn't keep up with the plot, but enjoyed getting out of the house. Also, he watched a lot of television. Laura sat through the same show over and over again, but to Quinn it was as if he was seeing it for the first time.

After three years of caregiving, Quinn's needs as he deteriorated were so vast Laura could no longer physically handle him. They both had long-term health care insurance, and Quinn was able to enter a local memory care institution.

Over the next few years, he became unresponsive, unable to speak, and spent his days hallucinating. Her Alzheimer's support group became her lifeline. She was miserable and alone.

After six years of solitude, she'd finally brought up the topic of dating at one of the meetings.

The facilitator said, "This disease doesn't need to claim two victims."

Laura was only in her fifties, healthy, and likely to have a long life ahead of her. Her friends were all couples, and had tried to include her in their social lives, but she'd often felt like a third wheel. She didn't know any single, available men her age. With trepidation, she turned to the internet to find some companionship.

David's profile with a picture of his Aussie caught her attention. They shared similar outdoor interests, and of course, the dogs. David had understood her situation and considered her a widow.

Laura's three dogs barked at her with pleading expressions on their faces, bringing her back to the present. "Sorry. You guys are hungry." She tearfully hugged Wiki, whose muzzle was graying. "You and I are the only ones who remember Quinn as he was, aren't we, girl?"

What started as a pleasant trip to Yellowstone had resulted in yet more heartbreak with David's serious injuries. Survivor's guilt washed over her as she looked at Laila.

"And on top of everything else, now we've lost Jade."

Chapter Five

A REAL PIONEER WOMAN

The Creed of the Activist: Be relentless, Stand strong,
Never doubt that you will win
—Vincent Kennard

FOUR DAYS MISSING—On her day off from her reservationist's job at Yellowstone National Park, Kat Brekken ate breakfast surrounded by her fur family. Rescued dogs Kris and Jake were on alert for any scraps she might drop. Her cats, Kiki and twenty-two-pound Hoss, named for the TV *Bonanza* giant, purred in the corner. The summer mornings were rarely balmy in Gardiner, Montana, a mile above sea level, but her home was cozy and warm. She ran her hand through her short cap of brown hair. Her frame was sturdy and strong, like that of her pioneer ancestors.

She frowned at the news in the *Bozeman Daily Chronicle*. One of her coworkers, Isaac, was missing. She knew him: quiet, well spoken, an educated young Chinese man who worked during the summer for a concessionaire in the park.

On Thursday, July 23, Isaac went backpacking with friends. He and his companions were swimming around noon in the Yellowstone River near its confluence with Hellroaring Creek in the northern section of the park.

They misjudged the strength of the river. Isaac suddenly struggled to stay afloat, pulled away from shore by the current. His friends stood in horror as he was swept downriver into a long stretch of rapids and disappeared from view.

An hour later, one of them got a strong enough cell phone signal to make a broken 911 call. Rangers immediately responded on horseback and on foot, but they didn't arrive at the remote location until two-and-a-half hours after Isaac had disappeared. They searched until daylight faded, and called off the effort for the day.

On Friday, a helicopter, two dog teams, and approximately forty National Park Service employees and volunteers actively combed the Yellowstone River corridor. There was still no trace of Isaac. Kat was saddened at the thought of the nice young man lost without a trace. Only a week before, they had scheduled a time when Kat could take Isaac wolf watching.

The next article caught Kat's eye, reporting the accident in Yellowstone on July 23 and the lost dog, Jade. After reading it, she checked Facebook. Her friend, Kristen, had shared a poster from the Yellowstone Visitor Facebook page:

MISSING DOG "JADE"
–Since Thursday, July 23, in Yellowstone National Park. My dad was in a horrible car crash and had to be airlifted to a hospital in Montana. Now my dog is missing so everyone please pray for her that she's okay
-Microchipped, wearing a blue collar
-If found, please approach with caution as she might be frightened from the car accident
-Please call/text Angie Sowers at....

The accompanying picture of the smiling black and white dog with blue eyes tugged at Kat's heart. Dogs had always played an important part of her life. In college, she adopted an older Irish Setter, Jess, because the dog smiled at her. Jess became her constant companion, well-liked by students and professors.

She and her dog took a road trip to Los Angeles in the 1970s. Kat pulled into an I-5 rest stop one Saturday afternoon. She used the restroom, and when she came out, a man approached her. He was clean-cut, wearing jeans and sneakers. There was nothing out of the ordinary in his appearance, or his demeanor. Nonetheless, Kat's instincts went on high alert, raising the hairs on her neck.

She'd trained Jess using hand signals, and she clicked her fingers at her dog. The large Setter emerged from behind a tree and ran to her side. The man stopped short, turned around, and got into a VW Bug. Relieved, Kat continued her journey, wondering all the while why she had felt so uneasy around the man.

Years later, the television displayed the arrest photo of a man purported to be the "I-5 Serial Killer," suspected of countless rapes and murders along the corridor from Washington to California.

She instantly recognized him as the man who had approached her at the rest stop and credited Jess with saving her life.

After college, she married and worked as a mental health therapist. Volunteering at the local fire department as an EMT/firefighter for seventeen years, she specialized in search and rescue.

She and her husband planned their future, buying a motorhome to take to sunnier climes as snowbirds. They lived frugally on one income in order to grow their savings to fund their retirement. Then, at age 54, her husband Lane suffered a fatal cerebral hemorrhage. In her forties, Kat found herself a widow.

She returned to her roots to help her step-grandmother in Idaho. Once her grandmother was secure, Kat took a trip in her motorhome to the Colter Bay campground in the Grand Teton National Park, where she was quickly offered employment.

The next year, 2008, she signed up for a summer at Fishing Bridge RV Park in Yellowstone. When she arrived, she stood outside her motorhome admiring the view. The sun cast a glow on the mountains and conifers glistened in the recent rain. She inhaled the scent of pine. Yellowstone Lake had been one of her favorite places in her youth. Settling near its shore, she realized she was home.

Kat decided to stay the next winter and found work as a reservationist in the park. That one season of beauty convinced her to stay in Yellowstone for the rest of her life.

Living in the RV made it impractical to replace her dogs after they passed away. In 2012, Kat was able to get a home in Gardiner with a fenced yard. Immediately, she started to fill the void in her life using the Pet Finder website to get a shelter dog.

First, she adopted Jake, a Border collie/Labrador mix from Boise Bully Breed Rescue. Volunteers had rescued the black puppy they found sitting by the side of the highway in Fairfield, Idaho. They suspected the dog had been abandoned when sheepherders left the area. He had an outgoing personality, and Kat immediately bonded with the energetic pup.

Then, in 2014, a friend contacted Kat asking if she wanted another dog. He had been impounded in Billings for over six months: if he wasn't adopted soon, he would be euthanized. Kris, a Finnish Tamaskan, resembled a wolf. His appearance made him suspect when found outside his fenced yard by animal control. His original owner spent over $500 in DNA testing and attorney fees to prove Kris wasn't a wolf-dog, only to find the Tamaskan had to be placed outside of Billings as a condition of release from the pound.

Horrified that the dog would be executed, Kat brought the huge dog home. To her relief, the gentle giant was soon accepted by her other animal-family.

The sound of a helicopter flying overhead brought Kat from her reverie. She knew search parties were looking for Isaac. At her age, she was hardly in a position to do a grueling backcountry rescue, much as she would like to help.

But, she thought, there was something she *could* do—no one was searching for the missing dog. Kat decided to drive to Norris and search for the black and white dog herself. "Come on, Jake." The big, black Lab mix's tail thumped against her leg. He might be her best chance to find the lost dog.

Her old pickup bounced along the unpaved street, and she turned onto Scott Street, Highway 89. Gardiner was a small town of 1,000 that provided tourist services to the northern entrance to Yellowstone. She passed the line of small stores and motels, most with pseudo-Western facades to appeal to the tourists. There was limited shopping, but she didn't need big box stores when she could thrill at the sight of a bison or moose meandering down the street.

Outdoor adventure providers offered guided fishing, horseback riding, backpacking, whitewater rafting, llama pack trips, and zipline packages. She winced as she drove by hunting guides who advertised trophy wolf hunting.

Once, she'd forced herself to look at the websites that pictured smiling people standing next to stiff wolf carcasses covered in blood, tongues lolling from their mouths—and she was nauseated. How anyone could enjoy killing these magnificent creatures for sport was beyond her.

She drove by cars with kayaks strapped to their roofs and RVs headed toward the north entrance of the park. Kat waved at every other car. Like any small town, some people got along with most everybody, and others held grudges. There was a general tolerance for the idiosyncrasies of others. She was just glad to be living in God's country, with easy access to the park.

She passed under the stone arch dedicated in 1903 by Theodore Roosevelt. The words FOR THE BENEFIT AND ENJOYMENT OF THE PEOPLE never failed to inspire her. Originally, it may have meant the spectacular scenery, the geothermal features, and the sheer wildness of an undiscovered country. Usually for her, it invoked the wildlife precariously protected in the confines of this wilderness. Today she was preoccupied with the thought of a domesticated dog alone in the wild.

She drove to the turnout along the Canyon to Norris road, three and a half miles east of Norris Geyser Basin, past Virginia Cascade. She parked and led Jake out on his leash. He walked along sniffing the ground.

Kat knew a dog's sense of smell was much greater than that of humans. Canines have up to 300 million olfactory receptors in their noses, compared to an average person's six million. Additionally, the part of their brains devoted to analyzing smells and interpreting them is forty times greater. Recent research indicated a dog actually "saw" with their sense of smell, recalling actual images of home, love, and comfort.

She scanned the area through her binoculars and mentally ran through the obstacles to Jade's survival. The number one requirement for the dog, fresh water, was readily available in a nearby stream.

Food was problematic. Garbage was fastidiously disposed of in the park. Long gone were the days when tourists were encouraged to feed bears from their cars or went for entertainment to the garbage dump to watch them feed every evening.

A dog in the wild, while preferring meat, would eat whatever it could find: berries, grass, and leaves. Perhaps it would hunt small rodents, find roadkill, or resort to buffalo scat.

Jade's worst option would be to attempt to eat the dead prey of a wolf pack. Wolves don't eat coyotes or dogs—their diet consists almost exclusively of elk—but they might kill any canine attempting to participate in the spoils. A dog also could be perceived as an invader of their territory, which wolves can defend to their death.

Then there was the unfamiliar wildlife. If Jade came upon foraging moose, buffalo, deer, or elk, Kat wondered which one of Jade's instincts would override the other—the dog's herding desire, or survival. Although the grazing herds often appeared docile to humans, like all wild animals they went to defensive mode if approached too closely. Only the previous week, a tourist taking selfies with a buffalo had been gored.

Humans presented their own danger. She flinched as cars went flying by. Jade would need to avoid the vehicles if she ventured onto the road. Speeding cars hit many animals, including buffalo whose bodies were transported by the park to a carcass dump. The cars involved were often totaled, and towed to the service station in Canyon Village. She assumed Jade's owner's vehicle was there, waiting for disposal.

Kat knew all of this having grown up with Yellowstone in her backyard. Her ancestors had arrived via the Oregon Trail in the 1800s. Her great-great-grandfather settled near Soda Springs, Idaho and raised sheep. Despite being descended from ranchers, she called herself a "wolfer," dedicated to saving wolves from trophy hunters.

Now, she worried that her beloved wolves might kill someone's dog lost in the wilderness. She made a mental note to check with local wolf-watchers for the latest location of packs near the accident site.

With her dog's nose to the ground, she stooped to examine tracks in the mud. Jade's? They were about the size of a medium dog, but there were certainly other dogs in the area.

Encountering a grizzly was always a possibility in the area. Kat fingered her bear spray on her belt. She never went anywhere in the park without it. Most of the time, she made a point of never hiking alone, especially in the backcountry, restricting any forays into the wilderness to groups of two, preferably three people. The real danger was getting between a bear sow and her cubs. Grizzlies would also defend their recent kills, and if Jade attempted to eat their spoils, she would be in serious danger from the fast-running predator.

After a final scan of the area, Kat tugged on Jake's leash. "Come on, boy. We'll try again another time."

As they walked back to her truck, all she could think of were those haunting blue eyes of the lost dog.

The next morning, Kat returned to Facebook. She needed help to find Jade and added a post.

Kat Brekken · Jade's been seen a couple of times since the wreck, but too scared to come to anybody as of last word. Rescue attempts will continue...Hopes and prayers...

The replies came in:

I've heard the same about familiar articles left out. If there's another family vehicle she knows, the son may be able to camp out overnight in the vehicle nearby until she comes.

I know of a neighbor that this happened to near Star Meadows. You can also leave out its dog bowl (no food), human owner's clothing or its toys or special blanket. The dog came back to its things in a couple of days. We have the same predators in this area that Yellowstone has.

Another ten people expressed their concerns, and suggested flyers of the dog be distributed. They would all be sharing this information with their Facebook friends. The Yellowstone Visitors Facebook page had over 124,000 people who "liked" it. There were close to 4,000 permanent and seasonal employees at Yellowstone, and Yellowstone Hiking had over 6,400 members.

Kat Brekken · Sharing on YNP Employees and hiker's pages.... Prayers are going up as I type...this area is thick with bears and occasional wolves.

Chapter Six

ANGIE AND SCOTT'S TRIP
TO YELLOWSTONE

FIVE DAYS MISSING—On July 26, David's son, Scott, posted on his Facebook page:

> **Scott Sowers** · I know it's a long shot, but if anyone I know is in Yellowstone National Park could you keep a lookout for our dog, Jade? My dad was in a car accident up there on Thursday and Jade ran away while he was at the hospital. Any help is appreciated. Reward if she's found.

Scott followed the post with his sister Angie's Instagram plea. Within minutes, he had twelve comments wishing him and his dad the best, and 79 likes from friends. It had been shared 2,010 times.

His previous post on the morning of July 23, the day of the accident, had been a wish for snow season. Scott enjoyed the outdoors at all times of the year, but he loved skiing best of all. He had his dream job at the Crested Butte Ski Resort, with unlimited time on the slopes. The town itself was filled with historic mining cabins, Victorian Painted Ladies, shops owned by locals, and quirky buildings covered in license plates. Almost everyone walked or biked around to their favorite hangouts, and it was a small enough place to know everyone.

Scott was using his vacation time despite the fact he had planned to attend a large going away party for a couple moving to London, England. He'd had to cancel all of his plans in order to search for Jade during his birthday week. He didn't hesitate to do so for his dad, with whom he was especially close.

On July 28, Angie Sowers drove I-70 from her home in the Denver suburb of Highlands Ranch to meet her brother in Breckenridge. She fretted about Jade, as much her dog as her father's. She was the one who had picked the puppy from the breeder's older litter. Angie admitted Jade was as stubborn as she was beautiful. Just the other morning, the puppy had refused to leave the car.

"I think Jade has ADHD," she had joked to David as Jade went from one toy to another, then back to the original one. Her dad had insisted she was nothing of the sort—his puppy was just intelligent and easily bored.

That was one way to put it, Angie thought ruefully. Recently their Aussie had started to exhibit the trait of picking up other dogs' toys in the neighborhood and bringing them home.

"Do you think they're souvenirs?" Angie frowned.

"Maybe." David winced as Jade shredded a toy, stuffing flying about the living room. "And maybe not."

Jade did love people and other dogs. Angie often rounded her up from the nearby schoolyard where Jade joined the kids at recess. The neighbors didn't complain when the smiling Aussie loped up to visit their own dogs. Of course, the missing and destroyed toys could change that if they ever identified the marauding thief.

The last few days had been a nightmare for Angie, seeing her father so injured, and not realizing what had happened at the time of the accident.

Now, she and Scott would both drive to Yellowstone. She could only spend a couple of nights as she had a long-planned vacation in Alaska scheduled on the 31st.

David had drawn a map to pinpoint the location of the accident scene, a few miles east of Norris. He had also printed out a pile of flyers of Jade. Thinking that David's scent might draw their lost dog in, Angie also had a couple of his unlaundered t-shirts and a pair of his sweats. Her friend had also posted a flyer for Jade on the Yellowstone Visitors Facebook page, and made this Craigslist plea:

LOST DOG YELLOWSTONE My dog Jade went missing after being in a terrible car accident. She fled the car once the door was opened by park rangers to get her out! She was last seen Friday morning in Yellowstone!!!! If you have any information, please contact me Angie Sowers....
BOZEMAN.CRAIGSLIST.ORG

Angie had also called all of the local animal shelters, alerting them to her lost dog and informing them her dog was microchipped. All of them promised to call if any dog met the description. Angie hoped it wouldn't be necessary.

She and her brother were sure they would find Jade right away, and she could bring the dog home to her dad. She mentally crossed her fingers. With her dad facing surgery for his injuries and unable to come back for weeks, she and Scott were Jade's best hope.

Scott followed his sister's car through the Wyoming landscape to Yellowstone. Until they got to the Shoshone National Forest, the stretch of highway was boring. It gave him plenty of time to think and to develop a plan to find Jade.

He tried to remember everything he knew about finding lost pets. His sister had brought along Jade's toys, including Jade's favorite plush Tweety bird toy, some chewing bones, and her dog food.

Scott recalled seeing Jade for the first time. His father had been so proud of the black and white Aussie with the blue eyes that he had brought the puppy to meet Scott at his workplace. Scott's coworkers at the ski resort office admired the cute dog with the goofy smile. Jade's butt wagged back and forth while running from person to person. Then, she squatted in the middle of the office...and made a pile of poop. His dad had run to get paper towels to clean up the mess, his face a bright red.

"She sure has a mind of her own," Scott said laughing.

That was still the case, he reflected. He wondered if Jade was anywhere near the site of the accident. Perhaps she hadn't come to his dad and Laura because she was so traumatized. She was nearly full-grown now, with the speed and agility of her breed. With her temperament, she might be miles from the scene. However, it was a place to start, he reasoned.

It was late when he and Angie arrived in Yellowstone. The entrance, fortunately, was open twenty-four hours a day, and the ranger directed them to the first-come, first-serve Norris Campground. The sites were nearly all occupied in the height of tourist season. Situated by the Norris Geyser Basin and the Gibbon River, the location was close to the scene of the accident. They pulled into an available campsite, shaded by lodgepole pines.

As they ate their Power Bars, Scott said, "It's too late to set up camp tonight. We'll sleep in our cars."

At an altitude of 7,500 feet, it was already cool. The weather forecast predicted the low temperature close to freezing. Scott lent Angie a sleeping bag and they settled in for the night.

Just as he was dozing off, Scott heard a rustling outside his car. Peering out, he spotted a bison. The massive beast strolled by, moving through the moonlight.

In the morning, they drove to the approximate place of the accident as marked on their dad's map. On the ground, close to a turnout/parking area, they spotted a piece of fabric.

As they neared it, Angie recognized the blanket. "This is Jade's crate pad."

They hung David's t-shirts and sweats on a nearby tree, scattered Jade's toys, and set out food and water bowls. Then they split up, calling for Jade. After a few hours, they questioned the approach.

"Could you hear me?" Angie asked her brother. When Scott replied in the negative, she admitted she couldn't hear his calls once they walked a few hundred yards away from each other. "This isn't going to work. If I can't hear you, Jade probably can't either."

They decided to walk the trails and parking turnouts, asking tourists if they'd seen Jade, handing out flyers to everyone they met. One couple reported they thought they heard barking and pointed in the general direction of the sound. Angie and Scott took off at a run, calling blindly for Jade. They ended up at a turnoff. In a parked car, with the window partially rolled down, a collie barked and whined at a couple taking pictures of the scenery.

That cold night, after hours of searching, they were discouraged and disappointed. Angie tearfully realized Jade has been exposed to the elements for over a week without any protection.

The next day they concentrated on hiking trails, stopping tourists to alert them about Jade, and posted signs in every nearby turnout, store, and rest stop. When they were almost out of flyers, they went to the Norris ranger station.

"We're the family who lost their dog," Scott explained.

The sympathetic rangers took a remaining flyer and made another sixty-five copies for them. They continued posting at every turnout, in stores, and at the entrances and exits to the park.

Angie watched as Scott made camp, expertly setting up his tent. Then, he lit a fire and they ate the sandwiches they'd picked up earlier.

In the twilight, the aroma of wood smoke wafted through the air.

"How many wild animals do you think are around here?" Angie stared into the darkening woods.

Scott shrugged. "Lots, I suppose. Why?"

"I mean like bears and wolves."

"I would think they'd steer clear of all of these people."

"There were buffalos roaming through here yesterday." Her chin jutted.

"Angie, do what you want to do. I'm going to bed." He moved toward the tent.

She opened her car door. "I'm no camper. I'll feel a lot better with metal surrounding me."

Scott had trouble sleeping, but not because he feared for his safety. He couldn't stop thinking about Jade. Had the Aussie been demonstrating her stubborn traits by not coming to them? Had she been so traumatized that this formerly friendly dog stayed away from all humans? Or was she just so hopelessly lost she couldn't find her way out? Was she hurt or even alive at this point?

The next morning, Angie stood by her car, ready to leave. "I hate to go without her. I wouldn't, unless I had to." She'd made firm commitments and reservations long ago.

Scott shook his head. "I have a couple more days. Maybe I'll get lucky. Text me when you get home, okay?"

As she settled into her car, she rolled her eyes. "Yes, big brother."

Scott grabbed his can of bear spray after she drove off. Ever comfortable with the outdoors, he decided to go bushwhacking, taking long hikes through the dense undergrowth off-trail. The going was slower, but he hypothesized Jade might be hiding in the brush, laying low from predators.

When he returned to his campground, he made a point of asking every camper if they'd seen Jade. If they didn't know about the dog, he gave them a flyer and her description. A family next to his site, with two girls around ten and twelve years of age, listened to his story.

"That is so sad," the woman said. "I really hope you find her and your dad recovers."

"Thank you. We're doing everything we can."

The girls looked on the verge of crying. "We'll keep an eye out for her, all the time."

The following day, Scott chose to focus on the more populated hiking trails and the open meadow.

One of the men he approached, after hearing his story, nodded in sympathy. "That really sucks, man. I have a helicopter. I'll take it up and see if I can spot her on my day off."

Scott wasn't sure if the noise would frighten Jade away, but he appreciated the thought. Discouraged, he went to the original scene of the accident, removed his dad's clothes from the tree, and collected the bowls and toys. Surprisingly, no animal had touched any of the food or water. He wondered if his human scent—or Jade's own scent—threw wild animals off.

After searching for a few more hours, he walked back to the campground. The family next door had moved on. They were such nice people, he thought. Lifting the tent flap, he spotted a folded piece of paper. It was a note from his neighbors:

Hi Scott,

Heard about your trip and experience through the campground host. My name is also Scott, so it is fitting you are in the spot we were in. We hope you are able to find Jade and your dad makes a speedy recovery. Know that all things work for the good, and you will have more time with your sister and dad. Cherish the time you have with them, for not one day is a given.

Scott,
I hope you find Jade and your mom and dad get well.
Love,
Sydney

A drawing of a spotted dog followed with the following note:

Sorry for your dog and your dad. I hope you can find your dog
and your dad recovers.
Hailey, age 10.

Dear Scott and Family,
We are praying for your family and the finding of your dog,
Jade.
May the rest of your journey be smooth and peaceful.
Holly Fitzpatrick

Inside it was a hundred dollar bill, "for your expenses in finding your dog."

On July 31, he made the long trip home to Crested Butte. It was a very different birthday from the one he had planned. His father was seriously injured, and Jade was missing. Every day that clicked by heightened his fear for the Aussie. Both siblings had thought finding Jade would be easy. Instead, they had driven home empty-handed.

There had been, however, an unexpected upside to the trip. Although Scott hadn't been able to help his father, the kindness of strangers left a lasting impression. He decided on his next birthday he would donate a hundred dollars to the local humane society to pay it forward.

The Facebook discussion of the missing dog continued as Scott drove home.

Kat Brekken · A couple of friends are planning to take their kids hiking in this area, in hopes of finding Jade and thinking that maybe, just maybe Jade will come up to a kid. Jade should be hungry by now, so treats are in store.

Chapter Seven

NIGHTMARES

Since the accident, Sowers' life has been a whirlwind of doctors, hospitals and trips to search for Jade. "This thing has put my life on hold,"
he said. "This whole experience has been a nightmare."
—Bozeman Daily Chronicle

TWO WEEKS MISSING—"It's a good thing I don't want to sire any more children," David joked to Laura as he shoved down the ill-fitting leg brace from Bozeman Deaconess Hospital. As he walked, it rode up and poked him in the crotch every few steps.

The brace caused only part of his aggravation. David's medication killed not only pain but also his appetite. It also affected his digestion, causing him to limit the pills and endure more discomfort. He could have tolerated the hurt a lot better if he had Jade next to him.

Jade always slept at the foot of his bed. By morning, she was nestled next to him with her head on his pillow. When he awakened, she would roll over and present herself for an extensive tummy rub.

Then, she would follow him to the shower and stand guard waiting for him to exit. As he towel-dried, she would help him along, licking the water from his legs and feet. He missed this morning routine the most.

Laura moved in to David's house to take care of him. Their relationship before the accident had been an occasional date, mostly hiking with their dogs, far from a full-time commitment. Now, she made appointments, drove him to doctors, hospitals, and surgery. She'd wrecked David's car, and even though the other driver had admitted fault, guilt gnawed at her.

She left her two older dogs at home, where they had access to her fenced yard, and drove twenty or so minutes to feed them twice a day. She had to keep Laila with her, who was at the chewy puppy phase, and would probably wreak havoc without supervision.

Laila arrived for the first time at David's house and ran about the kitchen, sniffing at the bowls and toys.

David's mouth turned down. "She's looking for Jade."

"We all are." Laura hugged him gently.

Not knowing if Jade was alive—she hadn't been spotted since immediately after the accident—added to David's stress. One minute he was hopeful, followed by despair, and underlying all, guilt that Jade had been lost in the first place. He tormented himself for bringing her along on the trip. At least he could have put her in a metal crate, instead of the plastic one that cracked like an eggshell.

He wondered what would have happened if they hadn't stopped to take that last picture or if he walked the dogs one fewer time. He knew his life would be an emotional whiplash until he could hold Jade in his arms again. Or accept the notion that she would never come back.

He had to force himself to sleep, afraid of his vivid nightmares of Jade lost in the woods. When his knee surgery was postponed for a week, it added to his deepening worry. He dreaded the operation, fearing his knee would never be right again. The recovery promised to be long and painful. David regarded his houseplants and garden suffering from neglect. He nodded toward the drooping tomato plants. "They look how I feel."

Laura couldn't do anything about his surgery, but she tried to lift some of his anxiety over Jade. "We both know Aussies are about the smartest dogs around."

David sighed. "She's freaked out. And no one will look for her like I can." He glanced ruefully down on his brace and cast.

"Remember my friend Linda's Aussie? She was smart enough to survive." The prize agility competitor had burrowed under the fence and disappeared for six days in the middle of winter. "Then once Linda made a plea on TV, they found the dog the next day."

David wasn't heartened. His son and daughter hadn't even been able to spot Jade, let alone get her. Angie had returned depressed at their failure, as had the usually cheerful Scott.

However, his kids had succeeded, in a way. The posters and social media were getting attention. The combined effort had resulted in several calls from people claiming to have spotted Jade. David would get a call from an unfamiliar phone number, and hold his breath as hope surged through him. "We saw your dog today." He'd do his best to get a description of the area, and tell the caller to report it to the rangers. He'd then call Ranger Page and update him with the latest information.

However, by the time a ranger arrived in the area, Jade was nowhere to be found.

"I don't want to send them on a wild goose chase," David said to Laura after a few of the calls.

"They want to find her too."

To take his mind off Jade, he spent hours on his couch, watching the National Geographic and History Channels. Once as he watched an episode on wild animals in the forests, a lioness took down a gazelle. He visualized Jade as the prey, running from wolves. He quickly changed the channel, only to find an ad for dog food, featuring a spry Australian shepherd. He shook his head, unable to distract himself from his thoughts.

His Aussies had always meant so much to him, constant companions who provided him with unconditional love. All he could feel now was emptiness where they had been.

On August 7, exactly two weeks to the day Jade went missing, David endured four hours of knee surgery. Eleven fragments of his kneecap were realigned and held in place with a combination of pins, screws, and wires, all corralled into a net. It was only, the doctor explained, a temporary fix; in about a year, the hardware would probably need to be removed. David was to hold the leg straight with a leg brace for several weeks, and then begin gentle movement. David would need extensive physical therapy, and most likely, a knee replacement sometime in the future.

Despite the severe damage to his knee, his dominant hand bothered him the most. The purple cast held his broken fingers in an awkward position. He was forced to use a computer mouse clumsily in his left hand while he attempted to work.

The insurance settlement was complicated. Four companies were involved for both of the vehicle owners and the two drivers. The funds for the replacement of his SUV were slow to arrive. Finally, he was able to get a rental vehicle so he had some autonomy. Laura had reluctantly let him drive her dog van, plastered with Australian shepherd bumper stickers. Since he had a good right leg and a working left hand, he could drive...sort of.

Laura drove David to the car agency when his insurance agreed to cover the cost of a rental car. With a cast on his arm and the prominent leg brace, he limped into the agency.

"Valid driver's license and credit card, please." The bored-looking attendant punched some keys on the keyboard, and the computer spit out the contract. Surprisingly, he made no mention of David's medical condition or ability to drive.

David signed the paperwork with his left hand in a shaking cursive, took the keys, and Laura drove him to the stall where the vehicle was parked.

She shook her head in amazement. "I can't believe it. It's not a problem that you can barely walk and can only use one hand."

"Not covered in the rules and regulations." He wiggled in and adjusted the seat so that he could keep his leg straight and still reach the wheel. He could do it, but just.

Laura needed to be apart from David the weekend following his surgery for her first AKC judging assignment after the wreck. The Mile High Agility Club of Boulder held the trials at the Schaeffer Athletic Complex's indoor arena. She was still in pain from the accident with sore ribs, back, and wrist.

Getting involved with the agility community had a profound effect on her: it turned her into a dog trainer, helped her to develop a closer bond with her dogs, and taught her grace under pressure. AKC judging also provided a much-needed income.

Her friends rushed up to her when she entered the indoor arena. Most of them had heard of her accident, and instead of hugging her, they patted her arm, relieved that she hadn't been hurt more in the head-on collision.

"Any other judge would've cancelled," one of them said and the rest agreed.

"Not in a million years. I missed you guys." Laura studied the setup with satisfaction. She took the opportunity to tell them about Jade, finding instant sympathy in those dog-lovers. Then she got down to work.

Laura started each trial by designing courses that followed the three F's: fun, flowing, and fast. She set up as many as twenty obstacles, often including a teeter-totter, a bridge-like dog walk, an A-frame, a table, tunnels, weave poles, and jumps. She likened it to putting a puzzle together: balancing the requirements of distance between obstacles, providing challenges, and yet maintaining safe angles.

The day of the trial, she measured the course to determine a time and checked all the equipment for safety. Other than the club's volunteer course builders, the layout remained secret. She went through the obstacles, assigning the order they would be taken at the last minute, giving no one an edge. All exhibitors saw the course for the first time and planned their strategy on how their dog was going to perform and how to run the fastest time with no faults.

While she judged, Laura stood in the middle of the ring. Her job was to assign a fault for the refusal by the participating dogs of any obstacle, dropped bars while jumping, or missed contact on yellow areas on the A-frame, dog walk, and teeter. The dogs must also stay on the table for a timeout of at least five seconds. She signaled any fault by raising her arms.

For this trial, she loaded up on Advil, and prepared for a long day. In most agility assignments, she stood while judging as many as 330 dogs and raised her arms an average of 700 times or more. By the end of any trial, her feet hurt and she was exhausted. She was pleased to see the level Astroturf floor in the big arena, which would be easier on her feet than hard packed dirt. It smelled better than the trials held in horse barns. As much as she found the aroma of horses pleasant sometimes, their odors intensified in the heat, giving her a headache.

The familiar sound of dogs barking excitedly in the background, combined with the electricity of anticipation by the handlers, returned her to a sense of normalcy. It was a hot summer day in August, with the humming swamp coolers taking some of the edge off the heat.

She watched as dog after dog attempted her course. With satisfaction, she noted the smiles on most of the faces of their handlers, challenging themselves and having fun at the same time.

On leash, an excited Australian shepherd at the start of the course jumped and twisted in the air. Laura's throat tightened as she studied the black and white dog. Unlike Jade, this Aussie's tail hadn't been bobbed. Instead, it had been left natural to act like a rudder and provide balance in agility trials. Even though the competitor didn't have Jade's rare blue eyes, Laura had to swallow hard and collect herself to judge.

At lightning speed, the dog charged through the tunnel. Laura imagined Jade in the wild applying the same Australian shepherd moves. The tunnel became the deep brush surrounding the meadow. As the dog ran up the A-frame, Jade climbed a boulder and scampered down the other side. She could picture Jade leaping over fallen pines as easily as the Aussie in the ring cleared hurdle after hurdle.

The dog in the arena moved swiftly and surely across the teeter-totter, but for Laura it morphed into an unsteady tree for Jade to navigate to cross a stream. The agility dog quickly ran the weave, easily switching back and forth between the poles, tongue hanging out. Laura imagined Jade, zigzagging at full speed, successfully eluding predators. The Aussie finished the course with no faults, and Laura could only hope Jade was doing as well in her trial.

Halfway through the event, a back spasm caused Laura to wince. At a break, one of her friends handed her a package from the drugstore.

"Try this."

Laura opened the bag and found a heating patch. She was touched that her friend had noticed. Apparently, the exhibitor wasn't the only one who had spotted her discomfort. Many friends commented they could tell she was in pain.

"I'm just happy to be back, doing what I love to do."

Holding an enormous ribbon, she posed smiling with the dog who had just earned his Master Agility Champion title, a huge accomplishment. To anyone who didn't know her story, she looked perfectly fine.

After the competition, Laura walked into the living room where David was stretched out on the couch in his Yellowstone t-shirt and sweats, watching a nature program on National Geographic. It was a bitter reminder of their disastrous trip.

She had brought home a pizza for dinner. Sitting at the kitchen table, she and David ate while Laila crunched puppy chow where Jade normally picked at her food, eschewing the dry in lieu of the wet.

"I really appreciate everything." Dave nodded toward the pizza. "It's just frustrating not doing things myself." Laura had bought protective covers for his cast and brace so he could shower, but getting dressed and undressed was awkward for him. He particularly hated not being able to cut up his own food, or bend over comfortably to tend to his garden. Most of all, he was trapped by his doctor appointments that kept him from going to find Jade.

"I don't mind." She fought back the wave of guilt as she watched Laila happily eating. David followed her gaze.

"I wonder what Jade's found to eat."

"Remember how she always found animal skulls and dead animal parts when we went hiking? She's got the intelligence; she'll figure out how to make them into dinner."

"That's true." David smiled. "She's young, smart, and strong."

Laura could picture Jade freed from the confining crate, instinct taking over. The will to survive was paramount: either fight or flight. She was probably frightened, unsure, hungry, exhausted, and on constant alert. She could be dodging coyotes, wolves, and grizzlies. Refusing to come to the rangers or tourists indicated she was definitely in survival mode. Would the hunting instincts of her ancient ancestors help her find food in the wild?

David interrupted her musings. "Have you noticed the date?"

She knew where he was going. "We've passed Yellowstone's record for a lost dog, haven't we?"

"Plus three days."

Then the phone rang. David looked at the caller I.D. It read, "Ranger Page."

August 13 Yellowstone Visitor Facebook page:

> Jade, the Missing Dog, was spotted alive on Tuesday August 11th near the Construction pile, one mile from Virginia Cascade which is between Norris Junction and Canyon Junction. There is a $500.00 reward offered.

Chapter Eight

SPEAK FOR WOLVES

"This year marks the 2nd Annual Speak for Wolves *near Yellowstone National Park. On August 7-9, people will gather in the Union Pacific Dining Lodge in West Yellowstone, Montana to hear about the need to reform wildlife management in America."*
—Official press release

TWO WEEKS MISSING—"Wouldn't it be great if we found that lost dog?" Sandy Monville was on the trip of her lifetime to Yellowstone for the *Speak for Wolves* event.

She rode with friend Nancy Warren, executive director of the National Wolfwatcher Coalition, whose mission was to advocate for the long-term recovery and preservation of wolves.

Nancy had been heartsick when she learned of Jade's plight from an early Facebook post by a board member of the Coalition, friend Kat Brekken.

"At least we have as good a chance as anyone of finding her."

They actually had a better likelihood than most people had; not only were they passionate about wolves, they were both seasoned animal rescuers. She and Sandy were on a 1,270-mile journey from the small town of Ontonagon, Michigan, perched on the south shore of Lake Superior, surrounded by wilderness. This area of the state is known as the Upper Peninsula, or "UP" for short. "Yoopers"—native residents—are familiarly kidded for their accents, and for adding "eh" to the end of a sentence. The UP had one thing in common with Yellowstone—wolves.

The two women were on the southern route through South Dakota, just outside the Badlands. That first night, they checked into a small motel with an attached restaurant. After getting a bite to eat, they noticed two dogs hanging around the parking lot. The skinny animals had ribs showing and were without collars. One sat scratching at his mangy-looking coat.

"They're hungry." Sandy frowned.

"Yeah. Well...." Nancy watched her friend go back to the restaurant. Sandy came out a few minutes later, carrying a Styrofoam container. In it was the dinner special.

"Here you go guys." Sandy set the container on the ground for the dogs until the food disappeared.

The next morning, when Sandy and Nancy left their room, they found several more dogs along with the two original strays staring at them.

"Apparently, the word is out," Nancy said smiling.

Sandy glanced at the restaurant, a closed sign in the doorway. "Too early."

They rummaged through their cooler and found some chicken and hard-boiled eggs, which Sandy fed the strays, trying to keep them from squabbling over the food. As they pulled out of the parking lot, Sandy started to cry.

"What'll happen to them now?" she asked her friend.

Sandy had a long history of rescuing animals. In early childhood, she always skipped up the road to her grandmother's house with small critters stuck in her pockets, like crickets and frogs. "What little jewel do you have for me today?" her grandma would ask with a warm smile.

Sandy continued her need to save creatures into adulthood, and instilled in her daughter the same love and respect for all life. They had once rescued an orphaned litter of baby skunks. People thought they were crazy, and they stunk when they delivered the kits to the wildlife rehabilitator, but they didn't care.

Sandy trapped abandoned cats and helped people find lost dogs. Whenever anyone called, she immediately hopped in the car, carrying her can of tuna hoping to lure the lost pet.

Her prize rescue, however, was Buddy. She spotted the hungry-looking stray near her home one fall morning. She was able to put food out for the dog, but he would run from her whenever she approached him. She, her neighbor Sue, and others continued to feed him throughout the long cold winter in hopes of catching him. Finally, one early spring day, he stood still, regarding her. Sandy noticed something was different. He allowed her to approach. As she neared, she realized his face was covered in porcupine quills. He whined with a pleading expression in his eyes.

"That does it, Buddy." She arranged a trap through the Facebook group "Lost and Found Paws of the UP." She caught him with a can of tuna and pork chops that very evening.

After a long recovery and extensive rehabilitation, her neighbor Sue adopted Buddy. He became a happy and loving pet, running daily to Sandy's house for special treats she saved just for him. The news of the rescue went around town, earning Sandy the nickname, "Dog Whisperer of Ontonagon."

Nancy had a similar love of animals. Born in Brooklyn, her earliest memories were of her mother rescuing unwanted pets. In their small upstairs apartment, they had cats, birds, turtles, and rabbits, but when her dad came home and found a dog sitting in the living room, he said, "Either the dog goes, or I do." The kids picked the dog, but they lost and her mom found a home for it.

Now that she and her husband owned 280 acres in the UP, she routinely found wolf tracks on their property and captured pictures of them on their trail camera. Their acreage, protected under a conservation easement, was managed as wildlife habitat. Along with wolves, they also shared the land with coyotes, foxes, bears, bobcats, and their prey.

As the women entered Yellowstone the next afternoon, they spotted elk, which had been reintroduced to Michigan after being hunted to extinction in the 1800s. They also saw herds of deer-like pronghorn, with reddish tan bodies and white rumps. Groups of bison meandered right next to the road. The goal, however, was to see at least one grizzly and some wolves.

The night before the conference, Sandy and Nancy met Kat Brekken for dinner. Up until then, Nancy and Kat had been corresponding through emails and on the phone. Their common interest in saving animals had quickly blossomed into an online friendship.

As they entered the restaurant, Kat nodded toward a flyer in the entryway. It pictured a black and white dog with a chew stick in her mouth. The expression in her alert blue eyes was mesmerizing. It read, "JADE was last seen after a horrible car crash on Thursday 7-23 near Ice Lake Trailhead. If you find her or see her please call Angie or report her sighting to the nearest ranger station." The phone number followed.

"Poor little girl. The family must be devastated," Sandy said.

"And to think it could be my Liebchen," Nancy added. Jade's escape from the airline crate had unsettled Nancy. She traveled everywhere with her German shepherd in the same kind of carrier, assuming the dog was safe. It was time to look for a better alternative, she thought.

Sandy grimaced. "My little Maddie probably wouldn't last a day." She pictured her miniature dachshund running through the woods on her short legs, stymied by the first big log.

Nancy knew even a large German shepherd would be frightened, and thought about how scared Jade must be. "I worry about the wolves."

Kat frowned. "Me too. We all know how territorial they are."

They traded rescue stories over dinner. Sandy shared her tale of Buddy and saving the skunk kits.

"Tell her about your intervention." Nancy suggested.

"Well...okay. I attacked a six-foot-six man who was beating a dog to the ground. My husband had to pull me off the frickin' bastard. I was ready to do serious damage."

Sandy banged her hand on the table, rattling the silverware. "Nobody, I mean *nobody* messes with animals when I'm around. I testified and the s.o.b. went to jail for animal abuse."

"And the dog?" Kat asked.

Sandy smiled. "Perfectly fine, adopted by a friend."

"Then there is justice after all," Kat replied.

As they finished their dinner, Nancy asked, "What about Jade?"

"There've been a few unconfirmed sightings in the general direction of Norris. She appears be moving away from where a bear and several wolves had been photographed near an elk carcass."

"Herding dogs are smart." Nancy replied. "At least she's lived this long, for what...two weeks?"

Kat nodded. "Almost. The record."

Sandy said, "We want to help."

"You brought binoculars, right?" When they replied in the affirmative, she said, "Good. We'll use them on the way to and from the conference to search for Jade."

The first day of *Speak for Wolves* was inspirational for the three of them; hearing the impassioned speeches warmed their hearts. Delisting the wolf as an endangered species in all forty-eight states could only have dire consequences, especially when it wasn't supported by the Endangered Species Act protocol. The need for action was clear.

Wolves were rescued from the brink of extinction in the 1970s. However, in 2011, the government turned over "wolf management" to individual states and removed them from the Federal protection of the Endangered Species Act. Soon, hunters in Montana and Wyoming were taking a total of more than two hundred wolves each year. Legal battles continued between the states and conservation groups.

Nancy set up a table for the National Wolfwatcher Coalition, delivering the message to the attendees. "For wolves to survive and thrive, I believe it is critical to dispel the myths through education. Those who believe no wolf should be killed for any reason do not help the wolf any more than those who want all wolves killed. It is up to us to educate the public to make informed decisions. Take the time to get the facts. Write a letter to the editor. Contact legislators."

National Wolfwatcher Coalition volunteers were scattered across the country but worked on issues in every region where there was a current population of wolves. Their goal was to find middle ground and encourage the use of non-lethal methods to resolve conflicts. Volunteers attended meetings, hearings, and workshops. They participated by providing testimony on a variety of topics including delisting, hunting, and trapping regulations.

All attendees agreed on one vital point: any move to delist wolves and allow trophy hunting along the northern border of Yellowstone could have heartbreaking consequences. Kat had seen the trauma of hunting firsthand.

Kat had become a fan of the great alpha female wolf of the Wapiti Lake family, nicknamed by wolf watchers as "06," for her birth year, 2006. The female bred with several males, probably searching for the right mate. She met two brothers who were half her age in 2010 and settled with them. Kat learned from 06 "anything is possible if one is determined to live life on one's own terms." She cherished every bit of knowledge shared about these magnificent sentient souls.

Then, on December 6, 2012, the great wolf 06 was shot and killed by a hunter outside the park. When the collar-wearing Yellowstone female was slaughtered, years of scientific study were lost. Out of the nine wolf packs in the park, five suffered losses from hunters.

No one knew exactly why the alpha female had wandered fifteen miles outside the park, into a legal hunting area. One week before, her pack mate 754M had been killed in the same vicinity. These wolves previously did not leave the park.

It was probable the male traveled outside of Yellowstone Park's protective boundary to search for elk in the tough winter season. Wolf experts theorized that the 06 went to find her mate. National news took up the story of Yellowstone's most iconic and famous alpha female wolf.

Kat had been devastated. She vowed to take action to prevent this kind of loss in the future. She spoke next.

"Killing wolves is costly. The wolf watching ecotourism industry brings multimillions of dollars to local economies. Examine alternatives and allow the families of wolves to do what they do naturally. And reap the benefits of a healthier land and a thriving economy."

Silently she added, "And wolves, please don't hurt Jade."

It was bison rut season. Over the next several days, Nancy and Sandy drove to and from the conference. Male bison strolled across the road oblivious to traffic, intent on finding breeding females. This caused massive traffic tie-ups—"bison-jams"—but the women didn't mind. Yellowstone's bounty of wildlife was the mecca they sought.

They slowly followed Kat to a turnout. Kat fingered her bear spray and grabbed binoculars to search the area for the Aussie.

"If we spot Jade, don't move toward her," Sandy cautioned. "Let her come to us."

"Do you have any of the owners' clothing?" Nancy asked. "The scent might lure her."

"No." Kat peered through her binoculars. "That would be useful."

They each carried dog treats that Kat had provided.

"Try to remain quiet," Nancy suggested. "The lower profile we keep the better. Hopefully she'll smell the food."

They stayed as long as they could, scanning for any sign of the black and white dog. After an hour, they regarded one another glumly. Discouraged, they decided to move on.

"At least we didn't see any ravens or magpies around," Kat said. "That means probably no carcasses nearby."

After days of conferences, interspersed with hours of looking for Jade, Kat took them to spot wolves in the wild.

Nancy was eager for Sandy to have the magical experience. While attending a wolf education workshop in Wisconsin in the early '90s, Nancy had seen her first wolf track. She had stared in awe at its size, nearly twice that of a dog. She wanted to share what she had learned about wolves and took home some scat to show friends and family, most of whom were underwhelmed with the hard excrement.

Nancy remembered fondly the time she and the group went "howling." It was a beautiful clear summer night, and for the first time, she heard a full chorus response, including pups. She had since heard wolves and pups howl dozens of times but she never tired of it. It was even more special when she was with someone who had never heard the cries and she could share their excitement.

Now, at the overlook in the Hayden Valley, the sky was tinted tangerine by the sunset. The odor of sage wafted through the air. Herds of bison thundered in the distance, sending up dust clouds. Sandy, Nancy, and Kat found a crowd observing something through their scopes.

"Over there," someone pointed out. "Along the ridge. That's the Wapiti Lake pack."

"Oh, I see them," another woman exclaimed.

"Where? Where?" Sandy had trouble getting the hang of peering through the scope, but she finally figured it out.

"I see a wolf!" Sandy had spotted the family of two adults and their four pups. She hopped up and down. "Beautiful, just beautiful." Her eyes filled with tears as she hugged first Nancy, then Kat. The other observers at the overlook, thrilled to be there for a watcher's first wolf, broke out in applause.

On their last day in Yellowstone, Sandy and Nancy were able to round out their wish list; they saw a grizzly with two cubs, and then a black wolf. They also put in hours searching for Jade.

Sandy had a hard time saying goodbye to Yellowstone—and Kat. Her new friend had regarded her while standing in the Hayden Valley and said, "I see you have it."

"Have what?"

"You have Yellowstone in your heart. It'll always be a part of you now."

Sandy hugged her. "You're right. I'll be back." She and Nancy hated to leave, but they both had husbands—and dogs—waiting for them at home.

"I'm only sorry we couldn't find Jade while we were here. Let me know what I can do to help long distance. Anything at all." Sandy gave her new friend one last hug.

Chapter 9

GREAT EXPECTATIONS

"Expectation is the root of all heartache."
—William Shakespeare

THREE WEEKS MISSING—Winter usually arrived in Yellowstone early and lingered. Snow could dust the peaks of the higher mountains year-round. Because of the weather, any road repairs needed to take place during the busy tourist season, much to the chagrin of motorists. Visitors suffered through the heavy congestion and slow traffic, finding the work an impediment to touring as much of the park as possible in their limited time.

Early in the afternoon of August 10, a roadwork crew moved equipment near Norris Junction. One of the workers saw a chipmunk make a hasty decision to cross the road in front of him, and before the man could do anything, it disappeared beneath the grader.

After he parked the equipment, he strode over to chat with his fellow coworkers. Something caught his eye as it moved through the trees. A black and white animal dashed onto the road, grabbed the dead chipmunk, and ran back into the forest.

He turned to the group. "Did you see that?"

When they nodded, he grabbed his cell phone and dialed the ranger station. After identifying himself and his location, he said, "We all saw that lost dog just now."

David set the phone down after Ranger Page's call, stunned. Jade was alive. The road crew had reported she was thin, but still very active and had sped away from them. Later that same day, she was spotted again, running beneath nearby power line poles. The ranger had waited to call them until he had more than one confirmed sighting in an area, and was cautiously optimistic she would come to her owners now.

He grinned. "Should we go get my pup?"

"Yes, yes, yes." Laura hugged him. "I can't believe it."

He noted the time—two in the afternoon. If he and Laura left immediately, they would arrive in the middle of the night.

"I don't think I can sleep in the car." He looked pointedly at his arm cast and leg brace.

"We'll leave first thing tomorrow morning. I'll call and get a room. How many nights?"

"As long as it takes," he replied.

The reservation was not as easy as she thought it would be. Yellowstone had just experienced its busiest July tourist season ever; rooms needed to be reserved a year in advance. When she spoke to the reservationist, he paused when she said she wanted a room for the following day for up to five nights.

"We're the people who lost our dog in Yellowstone in that accident."

The phrase worked. He asked her to wait while he found available accommodations. After an endless time on hold, he came back with a room at the Old Faithful Inn.

"Sorry," he said. "I tried my best, but that's about an hour from Norris."

Impressed that he knew where they would be searching, Laura thanked him profusely for finding any dog-friendly lodging for them. She turned to David. "It's amazing. It's like everything is pointing us back there."

They gathered what they needed to pack for themselves, Laila... and Jade.

Laura went to the garage and removed all of the stowed toys, bowls, and food.

David held the yellow Tweety bird stuffed toy. "Jade's got to be over her trauma by now, right?"

"People at least are seeing her. She might not be so afraid."

David stroked the plaything. "Let's hope so. I don't know if I can ever make another trip there if we don't find her this time."

The next morning, Laura loaded Laila into a spare wire crate that replaced the broken one. Now extra cautious, she secured it with a bungee cord in the back of the rental SUV.

In a festive mood, they took a different route to Yellowstone. The beautiful scenery mirrored their optimistic attitudes. After seven hours, they turned off Interstate 80 at Rock Springs. They traveled through rolling pine-studded hills along the scenic highway. They headed north through small western towns lined with pickup trucks and bars advertising package goods while displaying banners welcoming bikers.

As they neared Yellowstone, the landscape became more alpine, with peaks outlined by purple, crimson, and yellow rocky slopes. Rivers carved through the wilderness.

"This place is beautiful, isn't it David?" Laura gestured at the sign for the geological site *Gros Ventre*.

He tapped on his phone. "It's named for the Native Americans we forced from here. Apparently the name comes from a misunderstood hand sign French explorers interpreted as 'big belly.' Figures, huh?" He snorted. "We steal their land, but they get a park named after them as compensation."

Laura nodded to the beat of the music they had switched on. They rode in companionable silence for a while.

"We should have Jade by tonight." David grinned. "I wonder which dog food she'll choose."

"Maybe we should treat her first. What do you think, filet mignon? And Champagne for us."

"Sounds good to me." He stared out the window. "I'm sure she's ready to come home."

"Jade's obviously over her trauma. Even if she wouldn't come to strangers, she'll come to one of us."

They arrived around six that evening, after Laura drove for over ten hours. Summer was changing to fall. The grass was brown, and early morning temperatures were forecasted to hover near freezing. Her hands trembled as they neared the accident scene.

They decided to check the construction area, about four miles west. Next to the trailer that served as an office, a few men in hard hats lingered. There were at least a dozen pieces of heavy road-grading equipment, surrounded by piles of rock and asphalt. Laura parked and she and David walked up to the largest group of workers, introducing themselves as the couple who lost their dog.

"I feel for you, man. I know how much I would miss my dog." One of the men stroked his beard.

"I saw her," another reported. "Here and along the power lines."

"How'd she look?" David asked anxiously.

"Skinny, but she moved fast." A burly man pointed at the largest pile of asphalt. "Another time, she was right behind this."

"How much daylight do you think we have left?" David scanned the horizon.

A work-hardened man scratched his neck. "Maybe a couple of

hours. We'll keep our eyes peeled while we finish up here for the day."

Since David couldn't walk far, he set up in the SUV, calling and whistling for Jade with his good hand. Laura searched the nearby area with Laila.

The sun lowered in the sky behind the highest peaks, tinting the lenticular clouds crimson. Laura often thought these uniquely mountainous clouds resembled spaceships, and half-expected aliens to climb out of them one day.

Soon, the aspen groves would cover the mountains with swaths of gold. Autumn was usually her favorite time of year. A cool breeze set her shivering, reminding her of how cold and hungry Jade must be. She thought of David's beloved dog scrounging for roadkill as a chipmunk ran across the path. Laila lunged on her lead.

"Here puppy puppy." She'd read that using a dog's name loudly might make them think it was scolding.

"Come on, Laila, speak. Let's find your buddy." She'd been working with her ten-month-old Aussie to bark for a treat, hoping the sound of Jade's best dog friend might draw her. Her dog reacted to her command about 50 percent of the time.

Laura figured she'd been walking for almost an hour. Soon it would be too dark to search. As the shadows lengthened, the deep pinewoods started to take on a more sinister appearance. The dead trees killed in fires years ago littered the area like cadavers.

Then something rustled next to her and she jumped. Laila let out a low growl. They stood stock still, as Laura strained to hear. "What is it, girl?" She peered into the deep gray-green undergrowth, holding her breath. She drew Laila in closer.

After several heart-pounding minutes, Laura eased backward for a few yards, then speed-walked forward as fast as possible, calling out the entire time.

Relieved, she and Laila trotted up to the car.

"Any luck?" David asked.

"No." She loaded Leila into her replacement crate. "I think I'll stick to daylight searching."

Laura buckled her seatbelt with a wince. Her ribs had continued to hurt when she tried to sleep at night on her side. Still, she knew her pain was minor compared to David's unusable hand and throbbing knee. She tried to prepare herself mentally for the hour drive to the Old Faithful Inn. It was pitch black, and her palms were sweating when they arrived. Every twist in the road caused her to drive slower and more cautiously.

"If you keep at this pace, we might get there for breakfast." David arched a brow.

She only sighed. The more she worried, the less able she was to talk about it.

Arriving at the Inn, Laura tried to fight off a sense of foreboding. The immense log structure loomed in the dark. Projecting from the eaves of the main gable, gnarled log brackets supported beams. The porte cochere was recessed under the large portion of the central roof, along with a second-story porch directly above it.

They entered the mammoth building, with David limping and dragging his bad leg. Pain etched his face. He'd had knee surgery less than a week before, and was still suffering. His doctor had prescribed rest and told David to stay off his leg as much as possible. David had ignored doctor's orders yet again to search for Jade.

Above them, the seven-story lobby soared. A stone fireplace dominated a corner of the vast room. David pointed out a separate small landing near the roof.

"They call that the Crow's Nest. Musicians used to play there for guests during the early days of the Inn," David informed Laura.

"And now?"

"No one goes there since the earthquake of 1959 made it unsafe." He paused. "Except they say there's a ghost of a headless bride who haunts it."

A shiver ran through her. "Just what we need. More tragedy."

They checked in, identifying themselves as the "family who lost their dog."

"Oh yes. You must know someone; they found a room for you even though we're fully booked. And usually we don't allow pets except in the cabin rooms, but under the circumstances...I'll give you a copy of the pet rules." The receptionist eyed David's cast and leg brace, her face registering sympathy.

She explained they would be a few rooms from the entrance. "I'm afraid it's kind of basic." The shared bathroom was at the end of a long corridor. "We do provide bathrobes, though." She looked anxiously at the couple.

Laura thought of David limping to use the bathroom in the middle of the night. She pictured him going to shower with all of his necessary paraphernalia to protect his casts and brace. It wouldn't be easy for him.

"It'll be fine. As long as you have room for the dogs," David assured her. "We have one with us now, and hopefully we'll have two of them in the room soon." David beamed.

"Best of luck to you both."

They found their room down a long hallway. "This is pretty... western rustic." Laura eyed the room's log walls. It was furnished with a bed and a dresser. No television, no landline phone, no Wi-Fi.

"I'm just happy to have a place to sleep while we search for my pup."

Laura scanned the sheet listing Yellowstone's pet rules she'd been given at the reception desk:

Pets are prohibited in the backcountry and on trails and boardwalks for the following reasons:

Yellowstone National Park is a designated natural area where wildlife is free to roam undisturbed. Park visitors should be able to enjoy native wildlife in their natural environment without the disruption of other people's pets.

Pets occasionally escape from their owners. Domestic animals generally lack the ability to survive in the wild.

Yellowstone is bear country, and domestic animals (especially dogs) and bears are traditionally antagonists. A loose dog can lead a bear directly back to you.

There is a strong possibility that your pet could become prey for a bear, coyote, owl, or other predator.

There is a possibility of exchange of diseases between domestic animals and wildlife.

Thermal areas pose particular hazards to pets. Boiling water in pools and thermal channels can cause severe or fatal burns if your pet decides to take a drink or go for a swim.

Her hands trembled. "Maybe I shouldn't have read these rules." David glanced at the sheet. "They're only generalities."

Laura threw the pamphlet down. "They saw Jade yesterday. That's something, right?"

"Right." David peered into the darkness. "Let's get some rest. We have a long day ahead of us."

At first light, they awoke without an alarm. While David showered, Laura took Laila out for her morning walk. Apricot-tinged clouds streaked the sky. Laura's breath steamed in the air as Laila left paw prints in the frost-covered brown lawn.

"Your buddy must be cold," Laura said with a shiver to Laila, who wagged her tail. "Come on girl, let's go get Jade and bring her home."

As she drove to the construction site, Laura smiled. "If it could only be like this all the time. No other cars to slow us down."

"You got that right," David agreed. "Hopefully, though, this will be the last time we do this route."

She glanced at the empty crate next to Laila. Soon, she thought. Jade will be in it, and we'll be heading home.

Laura parked near the equipment, where several workers in hard hats talked and sipped coffee. She pointed toward the dishes she and David left the night before. "I know we're not supposed to leave anything out for her." The puppy chow was untouched.

"We left a couple of biscuits out ourselves," one man added.

"Hell," the big man said, "I'd leave a side of beef out if it helped you find your dog."

The couple thanked them, and started setting up in an area close by. Laura grabbed David's fuzzy royal blue robe and hung it from a branch. A worker let out a wolf whistle.

"Very pretty, man," he called out grinning.

David waved back, answering in a falsetto. "Thank you."

Laura then scattered some dirty socks and laid out David's favorite tie-dyed t-shirt, a true flashback to the '60s. She produced Jade's yellow, indestructible Tweety bird toy, arranging it a few yards away between bowls of dog food.

David sat on a log and surveyed the scene. Grinning, he said, "It looks like a yard sale."

The robe blew in the breeze like a scarecrow. Laura laughed. "It does, doesn't it?"

She sat next to him, smiling in the warm sun. Occasionally, David called and whistled for Jade. Laura fed Laila treats whenever she barked.

"I wonder why she showed up near here." Laura studied the busy area.

"Maybe the sound of people." The road crew's equipment rumbled nearby.

"You think it means security to her?"

"Probably." David glanced in the direction of the noise. "Wild animals wouldn't want to get too close to this uproar."

"Especially wolves," Laura agreed. "Although, if she ever saw one, Jade probably would stare down with her piercing blue eyes."

"And they would think she was the anti-Christ of wolves and run for the hills," David joked.

"Jade was always the smart one."

"Too smart for her own damn good. She's probably staring at us right now." David sighed.

Chapter Ten

DEATH IN YELLOWSTONE

Grief is a passage, not a place to stay. Grief is not a sign of weakness,
nor a lack of faith...it is the price of love.
—Author unknown

THREE WEEKS MISSING—"NO!" shouted Kat Brekken as she slammed her fist on her desk. Both of her dogs jumped. She stared at her computer screen in disbelief. Hoss, her giant cat, opened one eye and stared at her lazily. "Sorry guys." She took a deep breath. Her favorite grizzly bear, Blaze, had been trapped and could potentially be euthanized.

On August 7, in the middle of the *Speak for Wolves Conference,* a lone hiker failed to report to work at the Urgent Care Clinic in Yellowstone. After a search, his partially gnawed body was found in a known area favored by grizzly mothers with cubs. The deceased was 63-year-old Lance Crosby. Officials reported he was without bear spray for protection.

Kat had seen Crosby several times walking on trails. Once, she flagged him down. "Why are you alone?"

He'd shrugged. "It's how I roll."

"You know this is a well-known bear area, right? Lots of sows with cubs?"

He tapped his toe impatiently. "I live here and I know what I'm doing."

"At least you're carrying bear spray, right?" She never went anywhere in the park without the can hanging on her belt.

Crosby replied, "I feel I have more of an edge without it." He strode off, leaving Kat fearful and angry.

For a knowledgeable wildlife follower, it was easy for Kat to imagine what might have happened to Crosby. Blaze may have been surprised and threatened when the hiker had come up, possibly between her and her cubs. He may not have heard her warning bellow if he wore earbuds until she reared up, towering over him. He might have tried to run, the worst reaction, bringing on the bear's prey instinct. He likely put up his arms, trying to fend off the enraged mother sow, while she slashed at him with two-inch claws.

Kat and other wildlife enthusiasts had followed the over twenty-year-old female bear—a "sow"—for years. Blaze's human encounters had always been benign. She stayed in a popular area, raising her two "cubs of the year," an acronym of "COY" to fans. There were many photographs of the huge honey-colored bruin with the streak of white fur down her back, usually with her offspring playfully climbing on her or peering around her bulk.

Kat immediately wrote her own online post feeling dread and panic. If anything could be done to save the beloved animal, she had to at least try. She begged others to voice their sentiments to officials that Blaze was only defending her cubs, while the hiker had ignored the rules of bear safety.

Kat Brekken · Blaze's life well might depend on your input. PLEASE and Thanks!

It had been a bad summer overall for Kat. On July 1, the legendary African lion, Cecil, was killed in Zimbabwe by an American trophy hunter. On social media, Kat joined in the demand for legal punishment for the dentist whose guide had deliberately drawn the thirteen-year-old lion out of his protective preserve. Although the big game hunter was never prosecuted, he had been denied entry for hunting again in Zimbabwe. This did little to appease wildlife lovers against trophy hunting worldwide. A firestorm erupted on social media condemning the killing. His home was picketed and his office boycotted.

A record number of visitors flooded Yellowstone. The automatic budget cuts of 2013 had trimmed government funding by ten percent. This had translated into fewer seasonal workers and a freeze on all permanent hires. Existing employees were still feeling the effects, leaving them frazzled and overworked.

More tourists also meant more encounters with wildlife, some of which were potentially disastrous. No matter how many pamphlets were handed out and warning signs posted, some visitors continued to ignore the rules. As a result, in the current year five people had been injured by getting too close to bison while attempting to take photos.

Kat recalled a man who'd tried to touch a bison and was gored in the groin. "He's now singing soprano," she posted. "Darwin Award Candidates all!"

Recently one man walked up to a bull bison while his friend filmed the close encounter. Kat was furious when she saw the video. If the tourist had irritated the male—who was in rut—the incident could inspire an attack on another person hours later.

The worst event had been the drowning of her coworker, Isaac, Kat's sadness heightened by the fact his body was never found. She was sorry for his family in China who were unable to hold a proper burial or cremation ceremony. Grief seemed to permeate the three thousand employees of Yellowstone as they mourned one of their own.

Now, wildlife biologists had set traps in the area where Crosby had been killed, and Blaze was captured. If her DNA matched that gathered at the scene, the bear would be euthanized. Outrage erupted on the internet, wildlife supporters demanded help from their government representatives and park management. The man, they argued, had gone knowingly into an area where grizzlies and their cubs were plentiful. He'd been alone and totally unprepared for an encounter with a bear. The consequence of his actions would be the needless death of a mother defending her cubs as her nature required.

The incident came at a crucial time. Losing a cub-producing female like Blaze would hit the rebounding grizzly population hard. An online petition to save Blaze from a death sentence had over 142,000 supporters.

It was too late. Blaze was euthanized within twenty-four hours after the DNA test results. The officials felt they had no choice—once a bear killed a human, it could happen again and the public's safety had to be paramount.

In Kat's grief, she dedicated herself to saving the cubs. Another petition on the internet was posted, begging for the cubs to be set free in the wild after a stay in a rehabilitation center. Over 200,000 signatures supported this petition.

Nonetheless, the cubs were placed in the Toledo Zoo. Despite the zoo's great reputation, some of the wildlife followers felt it was a sentence of life imprisonment.

Kat found the decision less than ideal, but at least the cubs were alive. She knew the decision was a difficult one; the love of wildlife and the safety of humans had to be balanced.

Tempers flared as passionate advocates for animals were upset about the human-bear tragedy in Yellowstone. In an effort for peace, Kat posted a conciliatory message, asking for compassion for the Bear Management Team and the park supervisor. "Now is the time to come together and direct that anger towards being proactive to make life better for all."

Kat Brekken · August 15 · It has been brought to my attention, that some people have been so upset about the human-bear tragedy in Yellowstone, that they have forgotten this.... Many are hurting, and this includes the Bear Management Team. No Ranger signs up to kill any animal, it's not what they want to do. And certainly Dan Wenk cares deeply about this Park and all of the wildlife, including bears. To threaten people, who are working as hard as they can, to make sure they do the very best they can, is NOT ACCEPTABLE.

Kat paused at the keyboard. She thought of Crosby's family and regardless of the circumstances of his encounter with Blaze, she felt sympathy for them. She then added to her post:

Now is not the time, nor the place, to attack those who are hurting, including each other and the family of the deceased. Nobody wins, including those involved, bear and human. Yellowstone just lost some of its magic, and I'm heartbroken over all of it."

Kat realized she and the rest of Yellowstone had been experiencing the five stages of grief. At first, many could not believe Blaze was the sow involved in the awful incident, then anger started to inflame the situation. There were many who felt some good would come from the grizzly's death by bargaining for her cubs to go to a rehabilitation center. Now, a park-wide sense of depression seemed to set in.

In the middle of August, her dear friend, Corrine Nugent-Hayes, visited. Kat tried to make some sense of the tragic summer. As they walked, the distinct shape of a bear formed in the clouds, the sun shining through. Kat blinked back tears.

"Do you think it's a sign, Corrine?"

"The mother bear has awakened many spirits."

Kat decided at that moment she needed to do something to bring healing news to Yellowstone.

The lost dog had to be found.

She continued to search for Jade at every opportunity although she was losing hope. No one had contacted her about dog sightings in days. Perhaps there hadn't been any, and that made her even more hopeless. She thought of the family losing a member in the wilderness, with no idea where Jade could be at this point. Dogs were known to travel miles from the scene of their disappearance. She tried to convince herself the dog might have tried to get to the closest town, Norris, where she might be spotted. If someone brought Jade into the shelter, then the owners might recover her.

A frightening thought ran through her...Jade was as likely to have a confrontation with a grizzly as a hiker. She fingered the bear spray hanging from her belt as she hiked. Despite her depression, she noticed the park was even more beautiful and healthier than ever.

"*Slap.*" Kat smiled as the sound of a beaver tail hitting the water echoed from one of the newer colonies. Since the wolf reintroduction, elks migrated to higher ground in the summer to avoid predation, and stopped over-grazing willows along the rivers and streams; the beavers had more on which to feed and build their dams. As they prospered, the rivers changed course as the foliage returned to its natural state.

Kat had grown up in the era of animated films anthropomorphizing prey animals like fawns and rabbits. Fairy tales vilified predators such as wolves and bears. Over time, she realized there were no "good" animals or "bad" ones. All of the creatures who adapted to their environments were necessary in a healthy ecosystem.

Kat remembered Smokey the Bear warning, "Only YOU can prevent forest fires!" She railed at the phrase when newscasters suggested acres were "destroyed" in wildfires. Forests burned naturally, often set off by lightning. Some mature trees were lost, but the heat of the fire caused pine trees to release their seeds. Low-growing brush was eliminated, clearing the areas for renewed growth in the resulting sunshine. It was all part of the natural order of things. The Park Service now allowed the fires to burn freely until they became a threat to homes or structures, keeping the forests as natural as possible.

Wolf packs were reestablished to restore the natural order of animals. The Park Service did what they could to bring a balance between nature and humanity, a far distance from the '50s and '60s when wildlife was viewed as entertainment.

As Kat hiked, memories of her childhood spent in Yellowstone surfaced. Long ago, she'd sat by campfires in the evening with her family, staring up at the constellations in the clearest skies imaginable. Her dad had pointed out Orion whose "belt" led to the North Star, while the moon rose over the mountain ridge, the Milky Way a smudge on the horizon.

After her husband died, her first winter in the park had convinced her to stay year-round. She loved the peace of the place when wildlife ventured down from higher elevations and wolves sang to one another. Bison lumbered through the deep snow, silhouetted against the steaming geysers.

Now, inhaling the sweet scent of pines, she vowed to save her world. A cool breeze ruffled the leaves of the aspen trees, signaling the change of seasons. The sun lowered, and she knew it was time to call off her search. As was her habit, she studied the sky. Goosebumps covered her arms. The cumulous clouds resembled paw prints.

The next day, she received an email from a friend. Jade had been spotted by road construction workers on August 10 and several times afterward. Heart pounding, Kat called Ranger Page. "Is it true?"

He confirmed the rumor and told her the family was coming back to retrieve Jade.

"This is one amazing dog." Jade had survived over three weeks in the wild, managing to find food and water and avoid predators. The smallest seed of hope started to grow in Kat. "Let's pray Yellowstone gets some good news and they find their little girl."

After she ended the call, she reflected on the paw prints she'd seen in the clouds. She thought they had looked like a bear's at the time. Perhaps, she mused, they were that of a lost dog.

Kat Brekken · August 12 · I have a bit of encouraging news.... Remember the dog, Jade, that has been missing the past 3 weeks or so, following a car wreck? Well she has been seen near the construction area (not exactly sure, but think it's the road work between Mammoth and Norris), owner was contacted and my buddy just booked the owner a room and they are on their way. So keep those hopes and prayers rolling, as it looks like this just might have a happy ending. I must say, I am surprised, pleasantly surprised. Fingers crossed and smoke going up...

Nancy Warren · Fingers and paws crossed.

Chapter Eleven

OLD FAITHFUL

OVER THREE WEEKS MISSING—Three days into their current search, David and Laura arrived back at the construction site. The parked graders and backhoes glistened with frost in the weak morning sunlight, reminding Laura how little time they had left to find Jade before winter. The crew greeted them like old friends.

"Have you seen her?" David asked them anxiously.

When the workers replied in the negative, the couple decided to search by the nearest stream and drove to a turnout on the Virginia Cascade road. They reasoned that Jade loved the water, and it was a remote area away from the main road. David found a perch on a downed tree and whistled. Nearby electric power lines marched through the forest, where the trimmed brush beneath them created a natural pathway for wildlife—and Jade.

Laura and Laila walked back and forth beneath the lines for a mile at a stretch. Occasionally, she stopped. "Here you go, girl." She held out a crispy strip of bacon she had commandeered from the hotel's breakfast buffet.

When Laila barked, she was rewarded with the treat. Laura continually called out and squeezed one of Jade's squeaky toys. As the hours stretched toward noon, Laura heard desperation in her own voice.

Laila seemed to enjoy the hike as she always did, nipping at her leash and perking her ears up at the slightest sound.

Finally, Laura's grumbling stomach convinced her to return to David. As she neared, she heard his whistle, and then his hoarse call. Jade's water and food bowls were filled, her toys and blankets strewn about.

David held the favorite yellow Tweety bird, a nostalgic expression on his face.

"She really loved this one. It's the only toy she never could decimate." He turned it over in his hand. "It really looks more like a demented rabbit."

"Let's grab a bite, shall we?" Laura helped him into the vehicle and crated Laila.

They left the windows open as they yelled for Jade all the way to Canyon Village. They parked at every turnout, whistling and calling. At one of the busy stops, they saw something attached to a post fluttering in the breeze. David winced as he turned over the weathered paper. It was still legible enough to see Jade's smiling face and read the words they knew so well from Angie and Scott's flyers.

"This is killing me." David's voice quivered.

"Me too." Laura wrapped her arms around him and they both wept.

At the restaurant, they munched listlessly on burgers. Laura took a sip of water and said, "I wish I'd never seen that list of things that could go wrong with pets. I mean, I never thought about disease."

"I imagine wolves and coyotes get the same thing as dogs…distemper, rabies. Maybe parasites like worms and ticks."

"So if she survives, she may be sick." Laura's heart sank at the thought of Jade, skinny from lack of food, riddled with disease.

"At least Jade's shots are up to date. But, there's no vaccine for mange," he admitted. "Wildlife officials back in the day introduced it to get rid of wolves."

"That's terrible." Laura imagined Jade's beautiful long black and white coat, scratched off in large patches of bleeding skin.

They returned to see the wrecked SUV at the Canyon Village service station. It hadn't moved. Every crease in the crushed and dented front hood was outlined in chipped paint. From the open windows, a musty odor drifted from the soggy, ruined interior.

Laura peered in and caught a whiff of decay. The apples from their picnic resembled wizened old dolls. Fruit flies swarmed about the broken wine bottle. Brie oozed around green mold.

"It's even worse than I remember it." Laura stepped back, gagging. "I don't think we need to do this again."

David seemed too shocked at the sight of his ruined SUV to reply.

On their way back to the construction site, Ranger Page phoned. "Any luck with Jade?"

"Not a sign of her." David's voice was tense.

"That's too bad. I thought you had a fair chance." The ranger paused. "We can try food traps. We'll have to empty them at night." He explained many animals might go for the food, and predators could easily destroy the cages to get at the trapped prey. "That includes Jade," the ranger added.

David recoiled at the thought of his dog held in the trap while a grizzly tore into the cage. "If you keep an eye on them, I guess it's worth a try."

Later, they met at the construction zone and unloaded the wire cages from the ranger's truck.

"It took me a while to find these. Most are designed to trap bigger animals." Ranger Page stroked his gray goatee, scanning the area for the best locations.

Each trigger mechanism had to be carefully set. Ideally, as soon as Jade walked into the cage she would step on a plate that would snap the door closed behind her. The ranger covered the floors with pine needles and dirt to blend the traps into the surrounding areas. Finally, he poured globs of wet dog food into the bowls. Laura's nose twitched at the strong stench.

"We found pungent smells work best," the ranger explained.

David sat on a log, whistling and calling while Laura and Laila walked beneath the power lines. By late afternoon, she found herself weeping with frustration.

She wiped tears off her cheeks whenever hikers approached. She addressed them with her now familiar speech describing the accident and giving Jade's description. When they replied in the negative as to whether they'd spotted the pup, she pleaded with them to keep an eye out for Jade.

"There's a chance she's still alive." Laura hoped she sounded more optimistic than she felt.

The couple spent an uneasy night, tossing and turning. It hurt Laura to roll over on her bruised ribs, and David had refused to take his pain meds, hating the side effects to his digestion. At sunrise, they rose lethargically.

Laura watched David slowly gathering his things to make the trek to the public bathroom. She dreaded going to the same places with potentially no result. As David limped toward the door, she asked, "How about we take a short break this morning?"

He grimaced as he put weight on his leg. "Sounds like a plan."

After breakfast, they went out to the second floor landing of the hotel to watch Old Faithful. They sat on a wooden bench, while Laila gnawed a rawhide bone at their feet. Laura thought of their vacation only three weeks before. She had photos of David standing in front of the geyser, smiling, happy, and healthy. Jade and Laila had been secure in the back of the SUV.

David stared pensively at the growing column of water spewing up toward the blue sky. "Pretty much on time."

The crowd around them *oohed* appreciatively. They held up phones and tablets high in the air like a salute to the famous attraction.

The white steam cloud grew, merging with the cumulous clouds dotting the lapis sky. David reached over and held Laura's hand with his good one. "I want you to know I'm grateful for all you've done."

"It's my fault Jade's missing in the first place. Bringing her on the trip was my idea."

"It's not your fault, honey. We were in the wrong place at the wrong time."

She briefly closed her eyes at his absolution. She squeezed his hand. "Thank you."

He stared thoughtfully as the geyser continued its explosion, a gust of wind blowing the plume toward the west. "All this beauty is from the magma just below the surface. The supervolcano could easily erupt and kill us all."

Laila gave a sharp bark as the tourists around them chatted excitedly, snapping photos, and taking videos.

"With no warning." Laura shivered.

After searching all day, the couple returned to the Old Faithful Inn in darkness. The restaurant was fully booked for the night, so they bought a couple of cold sandwiches from the deli.

"They're kinda stale, aren't they?" Laura wrinkled her nose.

"Yeah." David threw down the half-eaten ham sandwich on his plate. "Laila's going to get the rest of this." At hearing her name, the Aussie's tail wagged and she yipped.

"I've trained her to bark for treats."

"Uh huh." David wore a disappointed expression.

Neither of them said it, but Laura knew they were both thinking it—Laila's barking hadn't lured Jade. Nothing had.

Laura took Laila out for her evening walk. It was a moonless, starless night. Once away from the hotel's lights, she had trouble seeing anything in the dark, including Laila.

"Come on, girl. Go potty." The leash loosened as Laila squatted.

Then Laila growled, and tugged hard.

The hair on Laura's neck stood up. Bison wandered the area, especially during the rut. She might walk right into a lone male, hunkered in the grass. Or other night predators.

"Let's go!" Laura ran, pulling Laila toward the distant glow of the looming, Gothic hotel.

As the couple fell asleep, a flash of lightning and a clap of thunder heralded a storm. They huddled together as wind blasted the old building with driving rain. The flashes and booms surrounded them. Laila, curled at their feet on the bed, jumped with every loud crash.

David hugged Laura tighter. "I'm so sorry for my pup out in the cold, with nowhere to go."

Laura's tears mingled with his as the sadness enveloped them.

As they searched the next morning, a quiet desperation took over. At breakfast, David had made a decision. They would leave the next day, Sunday. The bills from the hotel, the food, and gas required to drive almost one hundred miles daily were mounting. Every day was costing him money and lost opportunity to manage his business.

"We have one more day." He set his spoon down. "To use a sports analogy, we're in the fourth quarter with no timeouts remaining."

The rangers had emptied all of the baited traps. None of the food in the bowls scattered around the site had been touched. The toys appeared undisturbed. David's soaked blue bathrobe hung on the drooping pine branch.

He walked over and picked up his soggy tie-dyed t-shirt and wrung it out. "Maybe I should wave this in surrender."

At first light Sunday morning, Laura retraced their route from

Old Faithful. Graders and grinders stood mute in the deserted work zone. All of the items set out to lure Jade were as they'd left them. Laura silently gathered them and loaded the back seat. She carefully took down David's robe, smoothing its soft, damp pile. David lifted Jade's carrier blanket, rolled it into a ball, and threw it into the back of the SUV.

Neither of them spoke.

Laura picked up a toy and gave it a squeak. Laila barked, and Laura and David peered anxiously into the sun-dappled forest.

"You might call this the Hail Mary pass." Laura realized she was holding her breath.

"Yeah. Too bad we're not John Elway." David frowned, and limped back to the vehicle.

Following a pickup truck down a bumpy road under construction, they both jumped at a loud *crack*.

"What the...?" In front of David, a large star-shaped fracture appeared on the windshield.

Laura pointed ahead. "Must've been a stone thrown up by that truck."

"I'll owe for a broken windshield when we return this. I wonder how much extra that'll cost."

They wound their way south out of Yellowstone on Highway 191 toward Jackson, Wyoming, through stands of lodgepole pines. As they followed the meandering Snake River, the summits of the Teton Range appeared. The granite peaks jutted into the clear blue sky, while forests carpeted the lower mountainsides. In the foreground, split rail fences zigzagged next to the road, surrounding old wooden barns and log cabins. At Jackson Lake, the mirror image of the mountains reflected in the tranquil water.

It's like driving in a postcard, Laura thought. If only I could appreciate the view right now. Instead, she said, "Maybe we can come back sometime."

David nodded but remained silent.

Neither of us wants to say it aloud, Laura realized. Jade is gone. We have to accept it. No matter how hard we tried, we have failed.

David shifted in the seat.

She knew he was depressed, anxious to leave the disappointment behind them. The road was two lanes, but she accelerated a couple of miles an hour.

Motorhomes, pickup trucks, and Harley-Davidsons cruised the busy road to Jackson. The highway gave way to streets dotted with upscale western-wear boutiques and coffee shops. At the four corners of the center city park, huge arches made of elk antlers marked the entrances.

Laura glanced at the gauges. "We'd better gas up here."

As she pumped fuel, she was surprised to see David climb out of the passenger side.

"Need to use the restroom?"

"Nope."

She gaped, watching him climb into the driver side.

"What the heck are you doing?"

He adjusted the seat to handle his braced, outstretched leg. "What's it look like? I'm driving."

She sighed and got back into the vehicle.

David was going way too fast, she thought, as he gripped the wheel with one hand. His explanation to her was he wanted to get home as soon as possible and away from Yellowstone and everything associated with it. Beautiful scenery and wildlife be damned, he couldn't care less any more. In fact, if he never saw the place again it would be too soon.

She held her breath as he swerved around another car on the two-lane road. The crack in the windshield fractured her view, turning the highway into a kaleidoscope. The scenery out the passenger window was a blur of green and brown. Memories of the accident flashed through her mind.

"Please slow down." He didn't seem to hear her. She peeked at the speedometer. From her perspective, it looked as if he was going nearly one hundred miles an hour.

A police car whizzed by in the opposite direction. Then she spotted flashing lights in the rearview mirror.

"Oh, this is just wonderful." David said as he pulled to a stop. "Just friggin' wonderful."

The young state trooper appeared taken aback as he eyed David's cast and brace. After examining the car rental papers and David's license, he asked the usual questions: did David know how fast he'd been going, what was the rush, how did he hurt himself in the first place, and did he want another accident.

David replied, "I lost my pup three weeks ago in Yellowstone. I've been looking for her for five days."

"Is that your dog?" The officer nodded toward Laila in the back of the SUV.

"No. My girlfriend's. We never found mine."

David started to add details, until the officer stopped him. He returned with the citation and explained how to handle the payment.

David handed Laura the ticket as they switched places. While he stumbled back to the passenger side, she glanced at it. He'd been driving faster than the officer reported. Neither of them spoke much as Laura drove cautiously the rest of the way home.

At David's empty house, they unpacked in an oppressive silence. Laura started the washing machine and threw in the clothes they'd left out overnight, including the crate blanket. Laura hid Jade's other things in the same garage cabinet she'd used before. David might get a new puppy someday. That would be a long while. He did not believe another dog could take Jade's place.

David eased onto his couch with the television tuned to the History Channel. He propped up his leg on a couple of pillows, and pain etched his face. In his good hand, he held Jade's Tweety bird, turning it over and over.

Laura's phone rang as she went to sit down next to him. Puzzled at the Wyoming area code, she answered it. It was the Old Faithful Inn reservationist, who needed her permission to give out her phone number. Someone in the park wanted to speak to the family about searching for their lost dog.

The woman's name, he told Laura, was Kat Brekken.

Chapter Twelve

"WE HAVE TO FIND THIS LITTLE GIRL."

Compassion hurts. When you feel connected to everything,
you also feel responsible for everything. You cannot turn away.
Your destiny is bound to the destinies of others.
—Andrew Boyd

FOUR WEEKS MISSING—Kat Brekken was devastated when she learned Jade's family had returned empty-handed from their latest trip to Yellowstone. She gazed at her dog, Jake, who stared back with warm eyes.

"I can only imagine how they feel, losing their best buddy." She scratched him behind his ears, and he licked her hand. "I would do anything to find you. Anything."

Kat had been sporadically searching for Jade, occasionally posting on social media for help. Now that the family had failed yet again, she doubted they would be back soon. The rangers were overworked. Someone had to step in and take over the search if there was any hope of finding Jade before winter—if the dog could survive that long.

She dialed her friend in reservations, asking him to call the family and ask for permission for her to contact them. Hotel management had a strict privacy policy on guest information, but once she had the okay from her reservationist friend, she dialed Laura's cell number. When Kat explained why she had called, emphasizing her seventeen years of search and rescue experience, Laura put her on speaker and introduced David.

"She is one amazing dog to have lasted this long in Yellowstone." Kat paused. "Can I help you find Jade?"

The couple replied, "Sure." She heard the defeat in their voices. After all, the family had made several disappointing trips to Yellowstone in the twenty-eight days Jade had been missing. Kat wanted to give them hope again.

She pictured the black and white herding dog. "First, tell me everything about your Border collie..."

"To begin with," Laura interrupted, "Jade is an Australian shepherd."

"Oh." Kat made a mental note to get more details on the Western breed. Then she asked for more information: what kind of food did Jade prefer, what peculiarities did she have?

"For one," David said, "she's extremely independent."

"How old is she?"

Laura answered. "Fifteen months."

David added, "That's when she was lost. She's sixteen months now."

Kat did a quick calculation. In dog years, Jade was young, around the teenage mark for a puppy. Jade had youth on her side, but she lacked the life experience and wisdom of an older dog. Then again, Kat asked herself, how many domestic dogs had extensive knowledge in the wild, no matter their age?

David told her Jade had been spayed. "Is that a good or bad

thing while she's loose in Yellowstone?"

Kat considered the question. Jade wouldn't go into season, and therefore wouldn't be tempted to mate with any canines—although coyotes and wolves tended to be monogamous unless they'd recently lost a mate. "I think it's good."

Laura added, "Jade is afraid of anyone wearing a hat." She explained how the Aussie had jumped and barked whenever an older man walked by them in a Stetson.

Kat had heard of this behavioral quirk. It often occurred when a puppy wasn't exposed to various situations during their imprinting phase. "I'll stay in contact and let you know if we see her."

David explained he couldn't drive up to Yellowstone on a whim. The last few weeks had been rough, physically, emotionally, and financially. He was in business for himself, and every lost day cost him.

"I understand." Kat asked for photos of Jade. She'd only seen the one on the flyers, but she had been impressed by those hypnotic blue eyes. At the end of their conversation, Kat added, "I promise you—I will search for her as long as there are sightings. We have to find this little girl!"

Kat wanted as many people searching for Jade as possible. She contacted *The Yellowstone Insider* and *Bozeman Daily Chronicle* to publicize the lost dog, and update the story that Jade had been seen as recently as the previous Tuesday at the construction site.

Since she had a few days off from work, she took to Facebook and posted:

Kat Brekken · August 19 · I'm asking for staff and local volunteers, who could possibly assist with any time at all to work this with me, including probable hikes. Please message me if you could offer some time Thursday afternoon, Friday (sorry golf tourney partners, got a job to do and will have to pass this year), and Saturday. Thanks!!!

Sixty-four people replied to Kat's plea. Many of them were hundreds of miles away and couldn't make it to Yellowstone to help with the actual search. Along with well wishes, they posted suggestions: scatter Jade's toys and some of the owner's clothing around the construction site, put out a rug or bed to help her feel safe.

One recommended contacting the U.S. Fish and Wildlife Service to have them shoot Jade with a tranquilizing dart. Kat knew of an instance where a dog had been out over a year and wouldn't go near traps. After feeding it for several weeks, they shot the dog with a dart when it neared the food. It bolted into the woods, but volunteers followed and rescued the dog after it fell to the ground, incapacitated. She viewed this approach as a last resort; there was a risk they wouldn't find Jade in the deep woods.

Sandy Monville, who had rescued Buddy after a winter in the Upper Peninsula of Michigan, posted:

Sandy Monville · Oh Kat – Wish I could be there to help as this is one of my things I have experience in. I am praying for you all to finally bring this baby to safety. Just remember...if dog is sighted...SIT DOWN! DO NOT TRY TO CHASE OR CATCH...have good treats for throwing out and let dog come in. The dog is in survival mode now and most likely will not come to people...food is your best bet. Do not look at the dog...keep low and head down...she may come in to get treats. Good luck to you all. Thank you for taking this on...

Kat replied to Sandy that Jade had survived by eating roadkill and had managed to overcome all the dangers that Yellowstone had to offer. She was convinced Jade deserved every effort to save her.

Additionally, she'd asked for volunteers on the Yellowstone Employees Facebook page, particularly if they had search and rescue experience. A new parkwide electrician, Kevin Torphy, responded he was trained in the technique, along with a friend, Patti Johnson.

On horseback in search and rescue, Kat would provision for several days, bring along medical supplies, and stay in the wilderness until she found the missing person. She had a perfect three-for-three record and she wasn't about to let the blue-eyed dog be her first loss.

The sunrise was a smudge of gold in the sky. Kat whistled her dog into the cab of her black 1991 Toyota pickup truck. She started the engine, flipped on the defroster, and Jake watched as she scraped ice off the windows. By the time she got back into the cab, the interior smelled like dog.

"Let's go get that girl, huh?" She'd brought her best buddy, and extra leashes, in case Jade might be attracted to a fellow canine. It was worth a try.

Her dog huffed, his breath a nimbus in the chilly cab. His thick, otter-shaped tail thumped on the seat, as if in agreement.

An hour and a half later, Mount Holmes and the neighboring mountains over thirteen miles away came into view. Today, she had scheduled a search between Ice Lake, Virginia Cascade, and the notoriously steep Blanding Hill. Until the road was realigned in 1957, it was the first part of the Canyon to Norris road to become impassable in winter. It was near the site of the accident, and not far from the construction site where Jade had last been spotted.

She led her dog out on leash and headed toward the small group waiting for her. Among them was Patti Johnson, who she knew from Facebook but hadn't met in person. Kevin Torphy identified himself as the electrician working on the new solar power system. She'd been told he was devoted to saving large-breed dogs considered unadoptable. A perfect candidate to help her find Jade, she thought. Introducing herself, she shook the hand of the tall man with close-cropped graying hair and matching beard.

"Pleased to meet you."

She detected a subtle lilt to his voice. Before she could ask, he said, "Born in New Jersey, and moved to Ireland when I was one. I've come here via the South Pole and Afghanistan though."

Her interest was piqued. "You'll have to tell me more about that sometime."

Kat explained the grid search while she handed out the topography maps of the vicinity she had copied earlier.

"Jade needs to be close enough to clean water at least twice a day. We'll concentrate our efforts near streams and rivers." Kat and the others overlaid their knowledge of the terrain—firebreaks, power lines, the cover, the open space—on the topo map. They then divided the area by individual, to avoid retracing steps and focus on the most likely spots where Jade would gravitate.

Kat petted Jake on his broad head. "The key is to think like a dog."

She handed one of her walkie-talkies to Kevin. "Use this to call me if you see any sign of her." The cell phone coverage in Yellowstone was sporadic at best.

She and Jake drove along the Canyon to Norris road. A tornado force wind had torn through the area in 1984, followed by the big fire of '88. Around them, small pines and grass had sprouted, renewing the forest. She had searched this area several times before, but it was close enough to Jade's last food reward from the construction workers to warrant another look.

She then headed east toward Virginia Meadows at the edge of the Solfatara Plateau. Her phone rang, and she glanced at the time—a little after eight thirty. A friend reported Jade had been spotted near the employee dorms at Canyon Village. If this was true, Kat and her team were over eight miles from where Jade had traveled. She knew a dog could easily cover that distance in a day. Her heart picked up a beat. If confirmed, it would be the first sighting of Jade in nine days.

Four minutes later, another call came in from a friend who had seen a flash of black and white near her cabin at Canyon Village just minutes before. She told Kat other staff members had tried calling the dog in earlier that morning, but it had run from them. Security had been notified, and they had called the ranger station to report the sighting.

Kat phoned the Canyon rangers. Two traps at the construction site were regularly filled with dog food by the Norris rangers. Could more traps be set in Canyon Village?

Kat was encouraged—Jade was still alive. The key was not to chase the dog at the location of the last sighting, but to predict where she would be going. It was just too soon to tell if Jade was commuting between Norris and Canyon. She posted an alert on Facebook for all Canyon Village employees to be on the lookout. Then she called Laura and David to tell them the good news: Jade had been spotted by reliable sources after nine long days.

This time, she heard the tinge of hope in their voices.

Kat then considered the new potential search area. Canyon Village had been named for the Grand Canyon of the Yellowstone, itself beautiful and treacherous. Twenty miles long, the canyon is up to 4,000 feet wide and 1,200 feet deep in places. The Upper and Lower Falls plunge hundreds of feet to the bottom of the steep rocky walls. A fall from the sheer edge—which had happened in recent years— usually ended in death. If Jade was lucky enough to skid down the sides, she would have great difficulty climbing back up the crumbling slopes.

Besides the dangerous topography, Kat also worried about the many canines near Canyon Village. Jade could probably handle a lone coyote, but an attack by a band of them would be fatal. The Wapiti Lake wolf pack summered only a mile or so away from the waterfalls at Yellowstone Canyon. It would be difficult for Jade to avoid an encounter and the outcome was unpredictable. She was young, a puppy, and perhaps they would view her with bemusement. Or, they would find her an interloper in their territory, and quickly kill her.

As Kat drove along the road, she passed an expanse of meadow dotted with grazing bison. It was buffalo rut season. She stopped. "I'm worried, boy. An Australian shepherd might try and herd them." Her dog's tail banged her leg and he sniffed at her pockets. "Uh uh. Those treats are for Jade if we spot her."

She considered bison, especially during this time of year, the most dangerous and unpredictable animals in the park. More people were gored by them than hurt by any other wildlife. People thought they were "cute" and "tame." The enormous beasts were dangerous animals, especially if their space was invaded.

As sunset approached, she radioed her team to call off the search for the day.

"Tomorrow, same place, same time, please." She told them she would go to Canyon Village first.

"I will do so," Kevin replied. "Luck to you."

"I sure hope some of your Irish good luck rubs off."

Kat arrived home late, grabbed dinner, and then sat at her computer. Her dogs slept at her feet as she researched Jade's breed on the internet. She knew, despite their name, Australian shepherds weren't developed as a breed in Australia, but on ranches in the American West. Kat smiled—both she and Jade were descended from ranching stock.

Although the Australian shepherd resembled a black and white Border collie, there were differences. "Aussies" were bred to herd cattle and horses along with sheep, so they were larger and heavier than collies. She noted Australian shepherds were also reputed to have stronger hunting instincts, as well as tendencies to roam. All of this fit with what Laura and David had told her.

As she surfed the internet, she lingered on one particular article. When Native Americans first encountered Australian shepherds, they called them "Ghost-eye Dogs," since Aussies often had eyes of two different colors. They believed them to be sacred animals whose brown eyes focused on Earth, while their blue, amber, and mixed-colored eyes could see into Heaven.

A chill went through Kat as she studied the newest picture David had emailed her of Jade. Kat was spiritual. Maybe, she thought, Jade's ghost eyes would help the Aussie see her way to safety.

No wonder Jade had survived this long in the wilderness. Not many dogs could. She might be that one in a million who would make it long enough to be brought in.

She rubbed her eyes and checked the time. It was almost eleven thirty at night. A new post appeared on her page:

> There is a Border collie mix dog at Colmeys Veterinary. It was hit last night between Chico and Arrowhead. Please contact Colmeys ASAP. It needs medical attention.

Kat's heart pounded. Could her friends have been wrong about seeing Jade in the Canyon area? This dog had been hit by a car over seventy miles north of the construction site, but in nine days, Jade could have made that distance. Then, Kat focused on the rest of the post. The owner information was on the dog's microchip.

She took a deep breath and typed, "Thanks, but the last names don't match."

Adrenaline battled fatigue. Kat dragged herself into bed around midnight. Tomorrow, she would meet her group at the Canyon Village service station at eight thirty, a two-hour drive from her home in Gardiner. She was tired, but had trouble getting to sleep. Every time she closed her eyes, all she could see was Jade's haunting sky-blue gaze.

Chapter Thirteen

HIGH-TECH AND DIRTY LAUNDRY

FOUR WEEKS MISSING—Kat addressed the half dozen people assembled in the Canyon service station parking lot. Their breath fogged the air; the freezing temperatures of the last three nights had set record lows. Some of the group were friends and coworkers of Kat, others were strangers to her. A girl about ten years old stood at the side of one woman. Two people were accompanied by dogs on leashes.

Kat pointed to the wrecked SUV, decaying and yet to be towed away. "This is the family's vehicle that Jade escaped." The little girl let out a gasp. "Don't worry, honey. Her owner was pretty banged up, but he's going to be okay. He and his girlfriend really, really appreciate your help."

She instructed them to wait for Jade to come to them if they saw the dog. "Most importantly, don't run toward her. If you're carrying treats, throw some on the ground. Then sit down with your back to her. Call me on the number I've written on the flyer." Kat looked pointedly at the group. "Take off your hats, please. She's afraid of them."

A few of them regarded one another with raised brows, but removed their knit caps.

"I've also contacted the rangers about setting up live traps in this area, since she was supposedly seen near here yesterday. I haven't heard back from them, though."

Someone spoke up. "Ranger Page is officially retiring at the end of the month. Though, I've heard he's sticking around to the fourth of September."

Kat nodded. "I know they're busy." The Canyon rangers' headcount was down by three: one position hadn't been filled for three years due to budget cuts, another had moved on to a new job, and one seasonal had already left.

"That's why we're helping." She handed them flyers, asking the volunteers to show them to everyone they encountered. "If they think they see Jade, have them call the Canyon Lodge front desk. They'll know what to do."

As she had done in the Norris area, she gave them copied topography maps, and assigned teams of at least two. "There isn't a ton of wildlife close to the Village, but it's possible to encounter some, especially as you move near the woods. If you aren't carrying bear spray, stay close to the buildings."

Kat saw the wince of pain cross some of the faces of her coworkers. She guessed they were recalling the loss of a coworker who failed to carry the potentially life-saving spray, and the resulting loss of a beloved grizzly bear and her cubs. "Let's find Jade and give Yellowstone some happy news!"

The little girl clapped a couple of times. "Go Team Jade!"

Kat smiled. "I like it. Team Jade."

The dogs barked and pulled on their leashes as the group headed off toward their assigned search areas. Kat stood next to the mangled SUV while Jake sniffed the wheels.

She wondered why Jade would choose to come to Canyon Village, with the most accommodations in Yellowstone. There were over five hundred rooms in the Canyon Lodge and cabins, and the campground had almost three hundred sites. Six employee dorms were scattered around the area, all within walking distance to the concessions where they worked. It didn't make sense that Jade was attracted to the area because of the crowds.

Her male dog then lifted his leg and peed on one of the tires. "Come on, boy, this thing smells bad enough already." She wrinkled her nose at the stench of decay drifting out of the open windows.

His tail thumped her leg. "But it doesn't smell bad to you, does it?"

She imagined Jake "seeing" with his nose. Familiar odors painted a picture in his dog's mind's eye, envisioning whatever the scent represented. Her dog was probably "seeing" the rotting food, the owners, even Jade. And of course, Jade could do the same thing.

"Holy crap." Kat gaped at the vehicle's interior. Could Jade have smelled the wrecked SUV from miles away? At some level, it made sense. Why else would she come in this direction from the scene of the accident?

Still, she couldn't yet discount the Norris location where Jade had her last known food reward from the construction workers. Her dog sniffed her treat-filled pockets. She petted his broad head, and slipped him a piece of cheese. "And we know how important treats are, don't we, buddy?"

She watched as her group fanned out across the area. An extra "set of eyes" wasn't always all that helpful. Kat had seen posts that actually mocked the term "trained search and rescue," as if anyone could find anything if they just applied themselves—after all, how hard could it be find a person—or a dog—in the woods?

The National Association for Search and Rescue keeps statistics for the likelihood a person will detect something in their search lane. Volunteers with no training find about 20 to 30 percent of objects. Trained searchers' probability of detection was more like 50 to 60 percent—double that of someone untrained. Aware of the odds, Kat was relying less on individual searchers, and more on their education to make them aware of the lost dog.

She and her dog concentrated on the areas south of the southernmost employee dorms near the Canyon Lodge, where Jade had last been reported seen. The mid-century lodging housed mostly seasonal employees. Automatic payroll deductions paid for their shared rooms and three meals a day at the employee cafeterias. In turn, the mostly college-age people had the benefit of cheap living and eating, planned recreational activities, and plenty of exposure to others of the same age and interests. It was a great way to pass the summer in one of the pristine wilderness areas in the lower United States.

Most of them, however, would be returning to school or on to seasonal jobs by the end of August. After Labor Day, even fewer employees and guests would be keeping an eye out for Jade.

Kat took every opportunity to speak to any of the employees as they lounged by their dorms, reminding them of the lost dog. She showed them the flyer, and told them they only needed to call the rangers or the desk at the lodge.

One of the young women pulled her hair back into a ponytail. "I think the dog is sleeping under a bench near here every night."

Kat's heart quickened. "If you spot her...."

"I know, I know. But I'm out of here in a few days."

Kat Brekken · August 21 · 2:34 p.m.
No luck this a.m. but will keep at it this afternoon and then again tomorrow

Kat drove back in the afternoon and met with Kevin at the Ice Lake Trailhead where she presented her theory that Jade was drawn to the scent of the family's SUV.

He nodded. "Makes sense." His brow furrowed. "What doesn't make sense to me is why Jade's not been spotted in the campground there, begging for food. I mean they cook around the campfire every night. My dogs would be there first." He currently had a rescued shepherd/Mastiff mix with severe hip dysplasia and an elderly Great Dane. Kevin had described himself and his wife, Elena, as the worst foster people ever: they always wanted to adopt the dogs in their charge. At one point, they'd owned six Great Danes and fostered two more.

"Do you think she's traveling back and forth, or has she moved to Canyon?"

Kevin studied the topography map. "There's a natural roadway for her under the power lines. I've done some hiking along them myself. She'd be able to see all around her and stay safe from the cars whizzing by."

"I just don't know where to focus our efforts. I'm torn." Kat explained two staff members had reported seeing Jade. The rangers considered this a verified sighting since the witnesses saw the dog at the same time.

"They were so encouraged," Kat added, "that they're going to set a couple of live traps out in the Canyon area."

"What are they going to use as bait?"

Kat shrugged. "I assume dog food. You're thinking?"

"Dirty laundry too, loaded with the owner's scent. The more used, the better."

Kat wrinkled her nose. "I'll make sure to have David double bag it."

Kat's dog snored on the seat next to her while she drove back to Canyon from Norris mid-afternoon on Sunday. She had run late that morning, and hadn't arrived at Canyon Village until well after nine. Her search group had dwindled to four. Still, there was no sign of Jade at Norris or Canyon. It was as if the more people searched for Jade, the more elusive she became.

Jake twitched in his sleep. "I'm always saying we need to think like a dog. Unfortunately, I believe you can read my mind a lot better than I read Jade's." He opened an eye and yawned.

Herds of bachelor elk grazed in meadows, their antlers shedding velvet in ribbon-like strips. Occasionally, one bugled its high-pitched scream in preparation for the rut. A chipmunk dashed across the pavement and Kat slowed to let it cross. From above, a raven swooped down next to her pickup.

"God, I wish I knew where to search."

The bird made a sharp turn, flying about ten feet ahead of her. When she slowed, it slowed. When she sped up, so did the bird. Kat admired ravens, which had close symbiotic relationships with wolves. In Native American storytelling, ravens were form-changing wise guys and tricksters who took advantage of both wolves and humans.

"Look at that crazy bird, boy." Directly ahead of her, the raven's powerful ebony wings continued to beat. She followed it for several miles until she had almost reached Canyon Village. It suddenly veered, and headed toward a large meadow. She parked at the nearby service station. "Never seen anything like it."

When she returned home Sunday night, she called David with an update, and the request for his underwear.

David laughed and agreed to do it. "It'll cut down on doing my laundry for a while," he joked.

What Kat really wanted was Jade's family in Yellowstone, searching with her. But she knew that was asking too much. Then, inspiration hit. "I don't know exactly how to do this, but I have an idea."

Before she went to sleep, Kat posted an update on Facebook. While they hadn't found the dog, she figured Team Jade had contacted hundreds of people who were now searching. Once she received permission from Xanterra, the facilities management company, she wanted flyers posted at all high traffic areas of Canyon Village: employee dorms, restaurants, rest areas, and the trailheads.

She also had one special request:

Kat Brekken · Does anybody know how to take off a recorded message from an iPhone 6s to put on some sort of gizmo to broadcast it? I have the owner's voice calling Jade, and this might be a huge help in getting a scared dog to go inside a trap. Anybody who can pick up where we left off this weekend would be so appreciated...I have to work this week.

Kevin Torphy responded. He had been contracted by the U.S. government to work on missile defense systems in the Mideast, which broadcast early warnings. He figured he could work out a setup to play David's voice. He proved it the next day, when he played the recording for Kat on his iPod with external speakers.

Three claps and "J-A-ADE!!! J-A-A-A-DE COME HERE! JADE!!" David's voice sounded raspy and desperate. Then he whistled, going from low to high octaves. Kat was delighted that the sound could be broadcast in lieu of the actual owner making the calls.

However, when Kat approached the rangers with her idea of the recordings from the traps, the concept was nixed. "Too invasive for the wildlife and visitors."

She was crestfallen. It had seemed like a breakthrough for attracting the skittish dog. But then, the ranger softened the official position. "However, if the sound doesn't remain constant in a single area and no one complains...."

When Kat told Kevin about the ruling, he said, "We'll go to Plan B." He described how he would use his setup and drive around Yellowstone broadcasting the call. "We'll cover more ground anyway."

"But I have to work the next five days. It's frustrating." Her job as a senior reservationist was in Mammoth Hot Springs, over an hour from Norris and an hour and a half from Canyon. By the time her shift ended, it would be too dark to get much searching done.

"*Divil a bother*, as they say in Ireland, not a problem. I'll take up the slack."

"Thank you." She was relieved she'd found someone as dedicated as she was to finding Jade.

That night, as she struggled yet again to get to sleep, she saw not only Jade's blue-eyed gaze, but the raven. Had it been playing the joker, pranking her with its aerial acrobatics, or had it been delivering a message?

The next morning, a visiting woman filled up her car at the Canyon service station. The air had a bite of autumn to it and her breath came out in white puffs. She happened to be a veterinarian, and was intrigued when she spotted a black and white dog at the edge of the parking lot. The dog remained motionless, alertly staring at her through the mist. As the veterinarian walked toward it, she surveyed the back lot, shuddering at the smashed vehicles.

She initially surmised it was a Border collie, but as she approached, she caught a glimpse of blue eyes and no tail.

"You must be an Australian shepherd, huh?" The vet surveyed the other customers filling their vehicles. "Which one is yours?" She knelt down while the dog took a step toward her, sniffing the air. Thinner than optimum, but better than the obese dogs she often saw. The owner should be chastised, however, for letting the Aussie run free against park rules and common sense.

She turned around and called out, "Hey, whose dog is this? Should be on a leash."

No one responded and when she turned around, the dog had vanished. She walked to her car shaking her head. Spotting a man walking toward where the dog had been, she assumed he was the careless owner.

Behind her, in the front window of the garage, was an overlooked flyer with a photo of a blue-eyed Australian shepherd.

Chapter Fourteen

A YELLOWSTONE CHRISTMAS

THIRTY-FOUR DAYS MISSING—

Kat Brekken · August 25
Merry Christmas to Yellowstone!! Yes, we celebrate 2 of 'em
here.... this one goes way back to the early Stagecoach days
of the Park, when some travelers were stuck in a snowstorm at
Old Faithful and since it was the 25th of August, they decided to
celebrate Christmas. It's also the time of year when many of our
college students have to head back to school and a great way to
end the summer season.

With emergency lights flashing, Kevin Torphy drove the
Canyon to Norris road for the fourth time that day. The broadcast
of David's voice boomed from the speaker precariously lashed to
his side mirror. It was a lame setup for a parkwide electrician, he
admitted as he reached out to steady the speaker. At least it was

working. David's loud whistle echoed off the surrounding hills.

Whenever traffic appeared behind Kevin, he moved to the shoulder and waved them past. Once, a park ranger vehicle filled his rearview mirror, and he half-expected to be pulled over and questioned about the ruckus. The ranger drove past him with a nod. Unless someone complained, Kevin figured he could continue the unorthodox plan to attract Jade. He hadn't even needed to use his Irish gift of gab to talk his way out of a bind.

When interviewing the construction workers earlier, none of them had seen the dog since the original sightings. Still, they promised to be on the lookout for her. A couple of them glanced at one another.

"What?" Kevin asked.

Hesitantly, one of the men replied. "She's been gone a long time, hasn't she?"

Kevin assured him there'd been a confirmed sighting of Jade just a few days before near the Canyon employee dorms. "But she might travel along the power lines and show up here again."

"You a friend of the owners?"

"Haven't met them." He saw the question in the man's eyes. "I would want someone looking for my dog if he was lost."

As Kevin walked back to his truck, he glanced at his watch. He had a long day ahead of him, and might be late for dinner again.

He remembered taking the day off work just last week. About to start performing the chores on his wife's "honey-do" list, he had checked the Yellowstone Employees Facebook page. He'd found Kat's plea for help, especially from anyone with experience in search and rescue.

He'd told his wife, "There's a missing dog in Yellowstone. If they don't find it before winter sets in...."

Elena Torphy had smiled knowingly at her husband. "Go. This all can wait."

Kevin pulled into a turnoff where visitors were taking photos of bison in the valley. A bull was chasing a female, who apparently wasn't interested. The huge beasts moved with surprising speed, causing *oohs* and *aahs* from the tourists. He estimated the male was close to a ton of moving lust. The female, roughly half his size, was the more adroit. The galloping pair disappeared from view over a hill. He snatched his clipboard and walked up to the group.

"Hello. I don't mean to bother you, but…." Kevin displayed the flyer, and then the full picture of Jade he'd printed out. In it, she sat in a haughty posture with a chew toy in her mouth that resembled a cigar. He explained the dog had been missing for over a month, but was recently spotted in Canyon Village. "Would you please keep an eye out for her?" He also instructed them to call the park rangers and not try to catch the skittish Jade.

A middle-aged man nodded toward Kevin's SUV, which was still playing the recording. "What *is* that?"

Kevin explained the theory the dog might be drawn in by the owner's voice. "Is it bothering you?"

"Course not. It's pretty ingenious, I'd say." The man clasped Kevin's hand. "I hope it works."

Plump elk in their sleek summer coats grazed along the Gibbon River. Kevin imagined it teeming with cutthroat trout, as he drove to Canyon Village. His goal was to distribute a thick pile of flyers at the service station, the epicenter of the search.

Kevin parked in the lot, and left the recording of David's voice running. He'd been told by Kat that David's wrecked black SUV, the supposed "scent magnet," had been towed here. Hopefully, the owner's calls would add an auditory attraction.

Jesus, Mary, and Joseph. He stopped short at the black Nissan, crushed like a can of Guinness. The owner had been "pretty banged up" in Kat's words. Across the way, a white pickup had a smashed front grill. These had to be the vehicles involved in the head-on collision.

Kevin calculated if both drivers had been doing the 45 mile-per-hour speed limit, they'd hit with double the force, akin to smashing into a brick wall at 90 miles an hour. It was a miracle that only the poor fella had been severely injured. The owner was damn lucky to be alive. Kevin studied the debris on the floor and visualized the jolt as the vehicles crashed into one another, enough to break the pet carrier into smithereens. No wonder Jade was traumatized.

After checking Jade's flyer in the gas station window, he meandered in, verifying that the postings on the doors of the restrooms remained. He chatted briefly with the attendants, who knew about the lost dog and promised to alert everyone who came into the station.

"Most of them pay at the pump," one warned him.

"Maybe they'll use the jacks." Reading their expression, he qualified his statement. "The john, the restrooms."

Outside, he taped a flyer to the dumpster. His goal was to put one on every garbage container in the village. His rationale was simple: people emptying the trash couldn't miss Jade's imploring blue eyes.

Next, he drove to the employee dorms, stopping in each of the lounges. The interiors were simple. In one of them, two charcoal sofas straight from the '90s were strewn with afghans like his Granny used to make. The couches flanked a Danish modern fireplace. No flat-screen televisions here, not even a big old tube set. He knew the rooms were equally Spartan, with concrete block walls, furnished with twin beds and cheap dressers. He and his wife had lived in the Mammoth Hot Springs dormitory when he'd first arrived.

He stuck a flyer on a bulletin board, and spoke to an older man reading a book.

"Just wanted to let you know about Jade, the missing dog." Kevin pointed to her picture.

His grizzled face spoke of years spent outdoors. "I know." He resumed reading.

"I hate to interrupt you...."

The gray-haired man set the book down on the couch with a slap. "You already have."

Kevin tried his Irish charm, and gave a large smile.

"Well, I was wondering. You look like you've been here a while."

"You mean I look old." His keen blue eyes regarded Kevin beneath bushy eyebrows. "Where you from?"

"New Jersey."

"That doesn't sound like any New Jersey accent I've ever heard."

"Via Ireland for the first twenty years of my life. I started here in February."

The older man harrumphed and crossed his arms over his ample girth. "Well, I've either lived near or worked in Yellowstone all my life."

Two young women entered the lounge, each of them wearing Santa hats with their shorts and t-shirts. "Merry Christmas!" they called out as they left the building.

Kevin was momentarily puzzled. "I don't get it."

"Yellowstone Christmas. There're all kinds of stories of how it started. One of the most popular legends involved a blizzard on this date." He snorted. "It never snows *that* much in August."

"But it does snow?" Kevin considered Jade walking through white forests and meadows hunting for food.

"Yeah. A bit." He went on to explain that the celebration went back to sometime after World War II. Early park employees were nicknamed "Savages," infamous for their end-of-season parties held on July 25.

"Then, it was called 'Savage Christmas.' There's a whole lot more we don't know. The rumors are the Savage drunkenness and...every-thing...got out of hand."

Even by Irish pub-crawl standards, the long-ago employees must have been quite the revelers, Kevin thought.

The old-timer smirked. "Eventually, park management cracked down, changed the name to Yellowstone Christmas, and moved the holiday from July to August to extend the tourist season. What else do ya want to know?"

Kevin could hear David's voice calling for Jade in the parking lot. "What are the chances we'll find the lost dog?"

The older man reached for his book. "At this point—zero."

Outside the employee dorms, Kevin replaced flyers on the dumpsters that had been either blown down—or removed. He remained undeterred by the geezer's response. He figured he'd spoken to over a hundred people on his search so far, and every Yellowstone veteran had replied exactly the same negative way without a single "maybe" or "perhaps." It might be better if he, a relative newcomer, wasn't cynical and remained optimistic.

Canyon Village was anchored by the lodge-like Visitor Center. Next to it, the sprawling Yellowstone General Store was festooned in twinkling fairy lights. He walked across the large parking lot into Canyon Lodge where a decorated tree glowed. Christmas carols played over the sound system. Signs advertised special holiday meals for lunch and dinner, which included a visit by Saint Nicholas himself. At the desk, the receptionists wore Santa and elf hats and wished him a Merry Christmas.

"Care for one?" A pretty elf offered him a platter of fresh-baked goodies.

Kevin decided Christmas in August was a good tradition, whatever its origin, as he munched on a tree-shaped sugar cookie. He noted the flyer of Jade posted by the desk, and asked if Santa and the elves were telling everyone who checked in about the missing dog. They assured him they were. Before he left, he grabbed one more cookie.

"In the spirit of Christmas." He was really getting into the swing of things he thought, brushing crumbs from the front of his shirt.

Kevin steered his truck slowly through Canyon Campground along the loop edged with RVs and tents. Through the tall lodgepole pines, sunlight dappled the road. Although Kat believed the wrecked SUV should be the focus of the search, he maintained cooking odors from campfire bacon or burgers should draw Jade. *His* dogs would be first in line for a tasty treat.

When he spotted campers lounging at their picnic table or on lawn chairs, he drew his truck to a halt and approached them, clipboard in hand. Finally, halfway through the almost three hundred sites, one couple responded to his picture of Jade.

"Yep. That's the one we saw, isn't it, Betty?" He pointed toward the woods. "Right over there."

The woman nodded her head. "Yes, that's why we called the number on the flyer."

Kevin's eyes widened. "When did this happen?"

The woman frowned as she glanced at her husband. "Just this morning, right, Bob?"

Kevin phoned Kat to ask if she'd heard the news. She hadn't contacted him since the sightings weren't confirmed by at least two unrelated individuals. David and Laura had received several calls in the last few days. She cautioned, there were plenty of dead ends too.

Kevin decided to visit the campground hosts, the Park Service's volunteer representatives. He knocked on the door of the RV, bedecked with a Christmas wreath. A pleasant woman answered the door.

After introducing himself, Kevin said, "The missing dog was spotted by one of the campers today." He pointed to the stack of flyers in his hand. "I was wondering if I might talk to you."

"Come on in. My name's Barbara."

Her husband inquired if Kevin wanted fresh-baked cookies. "They're Barb's specialty."

"Yes, please." Kevin balanced his clipboard on his lap. Small touches of domesticity surrounded him: a handmade throw, an embroidered sign that read, "Home Sweet RV." Family pictures lined the small shelves above the living room. A decorated foot-tall artificial Christmas tree stood in the corner.

"Very homey," Kevin offered as he munched on an oatmeal raisin treat, still warm from the oven.

"Thanks. How can we help?" Barbara's brows rose.

Kevin told the hosts his theory that the lost dog was hungry, and the campground was an open-air delicatessen. "We have a chance of finding her here." He handed them a bunch of flyers.

"Could you please hand one out to everyone you see?"

"Of course." Barbara smiled. She explained as campground hosts, she and Don made the rounds twice daily, mostly to check that campers were safe. Unattended campfires left smoldering could start a forest fire. Food and trash left outside might attract bears.

"And then there are dogs left tied up at campsites with nobody home."

A seed of doubt crept in as Kevin asked, "So, people might assume the barking is Jade?"

"A possibility," Don answered. "It's amazing how many people—even employees—don't follow leash rules."

Barbara's brow furrowed. "There's even someone who works in the park who has three Border collies."

Kevin swallowed hard. *Shite.* "Do you suppose those were the dogs the campers saw today?"

"I hope not," Barbara said, "but it's possible."

Kevin started the two-hour drive home in failing daylight, pessimistic for the first time since he'd begun the search. Perhaps the old-timers had it right. Who was he, a newbie, to presume a dog might last this long in the wilderness? By distributing Jade's picture and flyers, had he just confused the situation?

Part of him clung to the fact Jade was a young herding dog, and the breed's intelligence was legendary. As a lad, he'd watched Irish sheepdogs crisscrossing the soft green hills and valleys with deft sureness. Their owners, clad in hound's-tooth caps, thick tweeds, and Wellies, whistled and called short commands known only to their dogs. In response, the black and white collies adroitly gathered large herds and delivered them.

Jade obviously hadn't been trained to do anything of the sort.

Perhaps he should take time off from searching for the lost dog. He'd already spent hours driving around. His phone rang. Expecting a call from his wife, he answered, ready to apologize for arriving late for dinner yet again.

It was Kat. In an excited voice, she said, "We have another confirmed sighting." Yesterday, two people had seen Jade at the Canyon service station at the same time. A man reported seeing her in the parking lot, as did a woman who happened to be a veterinarian. She stated the dog was thin but active.

"The vet apologized for not calling right away. She assumed it was someone's dog off-leash. Then, she saw a flyer at her hotel and recognized Jade's blue eyes. We can focus on Canyon from now on."

Surely, the woman wouldn't have missed the posting on the door of the restrooms. "Too bad the vet didn't have to use the jacks."

"Huh?"

"The john...never mind." He smiled at the ruby-tinged sunset glowing behind the rugged mountains. "Happy Christmas, Kat."

Chapter Fifteen

THE LOST YELLOWSTONE DOG

THIRTY-SEVEN DAYS MISSING—

Yellowstone Visitor · August 25 · Search for Jade the DOG continues. Denver native David Sowers is expected to make a full recovery after being badly injured in a crash at Yellowstone National Park last month. But he was on the move sooner than his doctors would like, with one thing on his mind: finding Jade, his 15-month-old Australian shepherd. Jade ran away when rangers opened the door of Sowers' SUV. The crash had smashed the dog's plastic kennel to bits, and Sowers was airlifted to the hospital with several broken bones and a shattered knee.

– posted by nbcmontana.com. 327 Likes, 103 Shares

Kat smiled as she read the Yellowstone Visitor Facebook page, part of her plan to keep the Yellowstone community aware of Jade's plight. It was working, she thought with satisfaction. Confirmed sightings, like the one the day before, encouraged her that they were getting close to bringing Jade home.

She then scanned the online news before heading to work. The lead headline caught her attention, "Lightning starts fire in Yellowstone Lake." A 1,500-acre forest fire burned at Promontory Point. The accompanying photograph showed a plume of smoke rising from the lodgepole pines.

The article stated the danger throughout the park was officially labeled as "High" due to the dry August. As long as no roads or structures were threatened, the Park Service only monitored the situation, as forest fires were a necessary part of keeping the ecosystem healthy. Severe conditions might extend for several more days until a predicted rain event came through. Yellowstone wasn't alone—sixty-six wildfires raged across the West, some of them threatening homes. Kat had a high regard for the fire-fighters who risked their lives. Years ago, she'd been involved as a volunteer EMT and firefighter and knew the ordeals they often went through firsthand.

With the arid environment, wildfires were possible anywhere in the park, ignited by either lightning or a careless camper. She was thankful no flames threatened the Norris or Canyon areas, at least for the present. A sudden flare-up would put Jade in more danger.

On her drive from Gardiner to her work at the Mammoth Hot Springs Hotel, Mount Everts dominated the eastern horizon. The enormous plateau with sheer limestone cliffs towered over the Gardiner River two thousand feet beneath. In the summer, she often spotted bighorn sheep maneuvering its steep slopes, safe from predators.

The mountain's namesake, Truman C. Everts, was famed for being lost in Yellowstone for thirty-seven days in September 1870. Accidentally separated from his expedition party, the career bureaucrat had been a study in ineptitude. Myopic, he broke his eyeglasses the first day apart from the group. He then lost his horse and most of his equipment with it. He retained only the clothes on his back, an opera glass, and two knives. However, he misplaced the weapons a few days later.

Everts fashioned a knife from a belt buckle to replace those he'd lost, and used the opera glass to make fires. One night as he slept, his unattended campfire burned most of his hair before he awakened, and he had to flee the resulting forest fire. Snow, wind, and rain lashed him throughout the month, while he subsisted primarily on thistles. A search party found him emaciated and near death. When asked to pay the reward money, Everts refused, insisting he could have made it out by himself.

Jade's thirty-seven days in the wild had tied Everts' record, but in "dog time," she had been missing for two years. Kat imagined the young pup's struggles: finding food and water, and staying safe on the rugged topography. Yellowstone teemed with large animals, all posing a threat to a domesticated dog like Jade.

From the window of her office cubicle Kat spotted a perfect example of her fears. A bull elk stood on the lawn, rubbing his antler velvet in the grass. She estimated him at nine feet tall, and weighing seven hundred pounds. It was elk rut season, their bugling calls echoing off pine-covered hills in early morning and dusk. Occasionally, two males fought while tourists watched them from the dining room window. The standoffs entertained the visitors, but were deadly serious business for bulls desperate to define a territory in which to mate.

The elk were the main food source for the wolves of Yellowstone. It was dangerous even for an experienced wolf pack to bring down a healthy bull. More often than not, the alphas avoided them, targeting weak and sick elk. Jade wouldn't have a chance if she were the target of a bull's forty-pound antlers or his well-placed kick.

Kat's shift seemed eternal as she took hotel reservations while others searched for Jade. Finally, it ended. As she left through the hotel lobby, a multigenerational family entered. The youngest, around three feet tall, wore a black Stetson, cowboy boots, and Wranglers, topped by a silver star on his chest.

"Well, howdy, Sheriff." She walked up to the young boy. "How's it going, partner?"

The little guy beamed while the rest of the family grinned in the background. "Real good, ma'am."

Kat left with a smile of her own, offsetting at least a little of her frustration that today she hadn't been able to directly help with the search for Jade.

The same day, Kevin Torphy took the day off work to drive around the Canyon area broadcasting David's calls for Jade. Kevin had asked a more experienced park employee to come along to make more headway canvassing. Davey Wiley had moved to Yellowstone in the 1990s, after leaving a well-paying job at Harley-Davidson in Milwaukee. He told Kevin, "I have everything I *need* here."

He explained that while winter living conditions were tough, and money often scarce, the Yellowstone employees and volunteers made up for it with a camaraderie unlike anywhere else Davey had lived. "If someone needs help, you help, no questions asked."

"I understand." Kevin thought of his past mates in rugged circumstances.

As the two men walked the power lines, a haze of smoke from the forest fire hung in the air. They agreed Jade would have an easy go of the cleared walkway. She'd have good visibility from predators and stay out of traffic on the parallel Canyon to Norris road to the north. Scat littered the pathway, evidence of the many animals that used it. Small voles and chipmunks scampered across their path.

"I bet that's what Jade's hunting." Kevin pointed at a rodent hightailing it through the grass. "And possibly eating that." A green pile of bison scat steamed in the shade of a pine tree.

"Yeah...." Davey stomped through the grasses.

"What?"

He lowered his head. "I know someone whose dog got loose here once. As it ran away from him, a coyote jumped out from behind a bush. Another one followed. Nothing he could do, it happened so fast. His dog died within ten seconds."

"At least Jade's been seen lately." Kevin glanced sideways at him.

"Yeah. There's always hope, huh?"

To Kevin's ear, Davey's tone didn't match his words.

Kevin drove the familiar route from Norris to Canyon, spending extra time in the campground. David's call and whistle blared the entire trip.

"Doesn't that get to you, Kevin?" His friend nodded toward the sound of David's desperate voice.

"You mean, 'J-a-a-ade, J-a-a-ade'?" He had the imitation down pat. "No, not really. Sometimes I play it at home to remind me how rough it is on the owner."

"I hear you, man. I don't have a dog myself now, but I do love 'em."

They finished the campground loop and drove to the service station to check on the flyers. Kevin nodded toward the parking lot. "Have you seen the poor fella's vehicle?" They walked behind the station. "It's right over here." He stopped.

Broken glass littered the empty space where the black SUV once parked.

Kat's mind raced after she received the call from Kevin. Convinced the wreck lured Jade to Canyon Village, she phoned David.

"I didn't know when the insurance company might tow it away," he replied, his voice frustrated.

Kat assured him so many people were searching, she'd lost count. One of her friends in Canyon brought hot dogs to work every day, hiking before her shift and during lunch, trying to spot Jade while waving the meat in the air. Another had closed her store, Stop the Car Trading Post, to search.

"We are getting results. Jade's closer every day."

David exhaled deeply. "I know people are trying to help. My son,

Scott, got a Facebook post about a black and white dog found in Harriman State Park in Idaho."

That was over twenty miles from the scene of the accident, and closer to thirty from Canyon. "Did the picture look like her?"

"No, not really. There've been a lot of dead ends lately."

With the SUV towed, Kat knew there was only one way to get David's scent out to lure Jade, and she requested more dirty clothes.

"I'm convinced we'll see more of Jade now that's she's in Canyon." So far, the four live traps had captured a sleepy opossum and one irate fox. The Aussie, too intelligent for her own good, shunned the food. Kat visualized her sniffing cautiously, recognizing a cage, and having none of it. "It's catching her that's the problem. The traps haven't worked."

"And my pup's running from everyone, isn't she?"

"She is." Kat let the unasked question hang. David had been specific the other day when she'd phoned him. He would only return to Yellowstone when someone physically had Jade. Period.

David regarded Laura after the call from Kat. "I don't know what to do." His business needed him. "I can't keep taking time off work."

Laura placed her hand on his shoulder.

Angie strode into the living room. "Do I have a vote in this?" She flung herself on the couch, arms crossed. "She's only going to come to us."

David silently agreed with her.

Laura's phone ringtone played and she answered it.

"Hold on, I want to put you on speaker."

The three of them listened as the woman said, "I've seen your blue-eyed dog sleeping under a bench by the employee dorms. She's been there for a few mornings!"

Angie arched her brow at her father. After the call ended David looked pointedly at his daughter. "I'll think about it."

The next day, Laura went to David's garage to put some trash into the garbage can. She paused at the cabinet where she'd stored Jade's things. One shelf was packed with her clean crate blanket. A few cans of dog chow were stored in the corner. Neither she nor David had given up, she thought.

Laura understood David dreaded returning to Yellowstone. If he didn't bring Jade back once again, it would break his heart. However, David would always carry the guilt if he didn't try again.

As she pushed aside the huge pile of toys, she found the one she wanted. Tweety was dirty but so far indestructible. She too was fond of the Aussie, even though she thought the dog had been spoiled from the day she came home from the breeder in Angie's lap.

An agility judge and lover of the breed, Laura acknowledged Jade emanated the *je ne sais quoi* that earmarked a good agility dog. If the Aussie had been trained, she might have been a top competitor. Instead of winning ribbons, Jade had demonstrated the zenith of her breed by her ability to survive in the wilderness.

Laura slammed the cabinet door closed, resolving to convince David to try once more. Time was running out. They must go back to Yellowstone before the snow made roads impassable, and Jade either fell prey or starved to death.

Two days later, David received a call from visitors who guaranteed they had spotted Jade a mile and a half south of Canyon Village on a service road. As soon as the people called her name, she ran away. "She was thin, but fast as a bullet." David's skepticism started to fade. Perhaps these sightings weren't just another dead end leading to disillusionment.

On Friday, Angie, David, and Laura sat at David's kitchen table eating dinner. The aroma of cumin and sautéed onions hung in the air. David had made his "famous" chili with help from Laura. He was relieved to get back to some of his routine, even if he had to perform the tasks sitting down and one-handed.

David's phone rang and he set it on speaker.

"I'm 99 percent certain I've seen your dog! She was in the meadow across from the Canyon gas station. I saw her blue eyes."

After the call ended, Angie looked at her dad with a pleading expression. Laura did the same. The kitchen clock ticked loudly in the silence.

David set his fork on his plate with a clank. He was softhearted toward all the females in his life, including Jade.

"What time do you want to leave?"

Laura resumed her meal, a small smile illuminating her face. "I'll pick you both up at four tomorrow morning."

Chapter Sixteen

"WE'RE THE ONES WHO LOST THEIR DOG."

THIRTY-SEVEN DAYS MISSING—

Kat Brekken · August 28

Just got a call from Jade's owner and they were called by a woman that is 99.9% certain she saw Jade in the Canyon Village area today!!!! Going to try to get this girl home and am really appreciative of all the efforts by so many people to help in this almost impossible effort. I can't believe this pup has lasted in the Park this long, to tell you the truth. She deserves to go home to her deserving family. Fingers crossed and prayers going up!!!

Saturday morning, Kat Brekken drove to Canyon Junction as the sky turned golden behind Mount Everts. Jake was curled up on the worn seat next to her.

By 8:30 A.M., a swarm of volunteers had arrived and walked

the area near the service station. She waved and called out to Kevin Torphy. "Ready?"

"You bet." He sipped his coffee as he strode over to her. "I'll take the high road, and you take the low road."

Kat laughed as she strapped a speaker to her wrist. She would hang her hand out the window as she drove her route, broadcasting David's call and whistle. She pulled some cooked bacon from her jacket. "Want some?"

"Sure." He grabbed a slice and took a bite.

She slapped his arm. "Not for you, silly. For Jade."

Kevin grinned. "Let's see if we can get her for the owners."

She hopped into her truck. It rumbled and sputtered for a while, but the engine finally caught. "Boy, this poor old thing's days are numbered, I'm afraid."

Her Lab's ears perked as she turned on the recording of David's voice calling for Jade. His whistle echoed off the campsites, and Kat prayed no one would complain about their early morning wake-up call.

Kat had celebrated after she spoke to Laura last night—Jade's family was coming. David's "fresh" dirty laundry was on its way and should arrive shortly at the Yellowstone main post office. A volunteer would pick up the used underwear and deliver it to the Canyon rangers, who were ready to set traps.

She reached over to tousle Jake's velvety ears.

"Maybe we'll have her when they get here. What a gift that would be, huh?"

He sniffed at her pocket that held the bacon treats.

The streetlights in front of David's house glinted on Laura's Toyota Highlander. She, David, and a sleepy Angie struggled to fit all of Jade's toys, food, and blanket into the SUV, along with their suitcases.

"Did you get Tweety?" Laura asked.

"Of course." David held up the strange toy. "Good morning, Laila."

The Aussie wagged her tail. A spare crate for Jade sat next to hers.

Laura drove the now familiar route north. As the sun rose over the plains, Laura was filled with optimism. She and David agreed that since there'd been so many sightings of Jade recently, she must be over her trauma and would come to them.

Angie yawned and stretched in the back seat. "Are we there yet?"

A muscle twitched in David's jaw. "We're in Wyoming. Probably another couple of hours."

He sounded miffed to Laura's ear. She reasoned he hadn't forgotten Angie's remarks from the night before. After supper, Laura had phoned Kat to tell them of their plans, and she'd overheard David and Angie arguing in the next room.

"I'm staying until I have Jade, Dad."

"We're coming home no later than Labor Day. That gives us six days, max. I've got a business to run."

Angie had shouted, "I'm not leaving without her! She's as much my dog as she is yours." Then she'd gone to her room, slamming the door.

In the SUV, Laura let out a breath when Angie went back to sleep and David visibly relaxed again.

After waiting for half an hour in line, Laura pulled up to the entrance to Yellowstone.

Laura smiled at the female ranger. "Ranger Page called us and said our lost dog was sighted at Canyon Village area."

"Ah." The woman nodded. "No charge. I hope you find her."

"Thanks so much. So do we!"

As Laura pulled forward past the gate, Angie asked, "Where are we staying?"

"Kat left me a message we're to check in at Canyon Lodge. She found a cabin for us. We're lucky, the park was full." Laura mused that it was a blessing having a reservationist taking care of them.

"That'll beat sleeping in the car. My back hurt for days the last time."

David replied, "It'll be a whole lot more expensive too."

"Whatever." Angie snapped her chewing gum.

David looked annoyed, but remained silent. Losing Jade was taking an emotional toll on all of them, Laura thought. Once they found her, maybe things would get back to normal. Maybe.

They returned to the scene of the accident on the theory Jade was splitting time between Norris and Canyon. Laura rolled down the windows, flooding the vehicle with the scent of pine. David whistled and called for Jade. They passed a string of cyclists riding on the shoulder of the road, pedaling with sinewy legs.

As they rounded a corner, Laura slowed to a stop. Two bison confronted each other in the middle of the road.

"Aw crap. They're not moving." She glanced at the dash, calculating the remaining hours of daylight.

A bull, weighing at least a ton and six feet tall at the shoulder, tossed his enormous wooly head, and then lowered it. He pawed the ground and turned toward the van, challenging them with a stare. Angie pleaded from the back seat. "Be careful! That buffalo looks like he'd like to run us over."

David groaned. "Get to the side. We're creating a bison jam."

Laura glanced in the rearview mirror at the cars lining up behind. "I don't think they want to pass me."

Tourists held their phones aloft, taking photos and videos.

"Maybe I should just drive through." Laura shifted the car into drive.

"No, Laura!" Angie shouted. She waved the pamphlet the ranger had given them. "Not what we're supposed to do."

"Honk at it," David suggested.

All Laura could envision was creating a stampede. "I'll guess we'll just have to wait." She watched the minutes tick by on the clock.

After a long standoff, the larger bull bellowed and the smaller male sauntered to the side of the road, yielding the massive male his prize of a female harem grazing nearby.

Two hours after their arrival in the park, Laura stopped her SUV.

Releasing Laila from her crate, they walked to the Ice Lake Trailhead, where something fluttered in the wind next to the bear warnings.

"It's a Jade poster!" Angie studied it. "Her picture's the same, but it's not the one I put up."

Handwritten notes were scrawled across the colorful printed flyer.

Recent sightings: *8/27, 8/28 Canyon Junction employee housing*
Jade is skittish following her recent trauma. DO NOT chase her.
TAKE HATS OFF—SHE'S AFRAID
DO NOT USE HER NAME. THIS SEEMS TO SCARE HER. USE "HERE PUPPY."

David shook his head. "I had no idea people were doing all of this."

Laura recognized her own phone number written in magic marker across the entire flyer. The dates of the last sightings were only yesterday and the day before. "We're wasting our time here. Let's go where she was last seen."

As she drove east on the Canyon to Norris road, David stared out the window toward the power lines. After a few minutes, he shouted, *"Pull over!"*

"Did you see her?" A rush of adrenaline prickled Laura's skin as she maneuvered the SUV to the shoulder.

"No, but look!" David pointed out the window. "A bear. It's pole dancing." He reached for his camera.

Angie let out a yelp. "Oh my God. This is what Jade's been running from. Let's go!"

A huge brown grizzly stood close to a utility pole. The bear moved up and down, scratching its humped back. Then it turned and swiped its long claws along the wooden timber.

Laura sat frozen, staring at the beast. It appeared to be seven feet tall on its hind legs, with a girth the size of a Sequoia. The power of the animal next to an Australian shepherd was hard to imagine. One swipe with the enormous paw could destroy a grown man much less a young Aussie.

David took a photo and laughed. "This is so cool."

"We're out of here." Laura slammed her vehicle in gear, and prayed Jade wasn't walking the power lines today.

As Laura drove east toward Canyon, David caught a glimpse of tire tracks leading into the woods. "I wonder if this is the service road where they saw Jade."

"Only one way to find out." Laura steered down the bumpy lane. "Keep an eye out for her."

They rattled down the tracks, sending up a plume of dust behind them.

"I'm not sure we should be here." Angie pointed to a sign warning of bears. "We just saw that other grizzly."

They bumped along the road for about half an hour when they reached a locked gate.

Laura parked. "This looks like the area the woman described when she called."

"Let's get out and take a look."

Angie voiced her opinion. "Uh uh. I don't sleep in tents, and I don't go outside with bear warnings all around me."

David swung around. "Well, don't come then."

Laura was torn. Part of her wanted to go with him, but Angie was right. The signs were there for a reason. She turned to David, questioning the wisdom of leaving the car.

Just as he opened the car door, his phone rang. "We'll be right there." He shut the door. "The rangers just spotted Jade in the meadow near the Canyon service station."

"Hold on." Laura made a three-point turn, then hit the accelerator hard.

"Whoa, Mario Andretti." David and Angie grabbed the roof bars.

"Hang on." Laura stared ahead.

The piles of stuff on the car seats levitated when she hit the next bump.

He turned to face Angie. "Usually, she does the speed limit. No more, no less." He grunted as they hit a large pothole, jolting them to the bones.

A huddle of rangers peered through binoculars in the meadow at Canyon Village.

Laura grinned. "Twenty minutes! Record time!"

The SUV had barely come to a halt when Angie charged from the back seat. David flung off his seatbelt and jumped out, landing on his good leg.

Angie dashed across the meadow toward the woods. David hobbled behind her calling and whistling for Jade. The rangers chased them, shouting, "Stop."

Laura grabbed Laila from her crate and raced after the group. Visitors parked their vehicles and stood gaping at the commotion. As Laura loped by them, someone called out, "What's going on?"

"Lost dog," Laura shouted over her shoulder.

Angie moved fast, but the rangers and Laura easily caught up with a limping David. One of the quicker men stopped Angie.

Once they assembled, the lead ranger addressed the trio. "That dog doesn't come if you shout or run after her. Most importantly, you can't go in the woods without bear spray. Several grizzlies have been reported nearby." He put cans into Angie and David's outstretched hands. Demonstrating how to use the protective spray, he finally agreed to let them go.

Laura took the ranger's advice not to chase after Jade. "I'll stay in the meadow." Laila tugged on the leash, attempting to follow David and Angie into the woods. "Keep together," Laura called out. She worried neither of them could pull out the safety clip and aim it at a bear quick enough, especially David with only one good hand.

Anger burned away fear as she heard David and Angie shouting

Jade's name; dammit, they were doing everything wrong.

The lead ranger joined Laura as her Aussie sniffed through the tall brown grasses.

"That's a shame. Someone just saw your dog. You must've driven right by her when you got here."

"That's been the story of our lives for weeks." A shadow crossed over them, cast by a raven flying toward the dark woods. Laura took out a piece of cheese, and Laila barked as she'd been trained. "We're hoping she'll come to one of us or her pal here. On the way from Norris, we took that service road, and then got your call."

The ranger stopped short. "How did you get in *there*?"

Laura frowned. "I saw the entrance and made a right hand turn."

"It should've been chained and locked." He explained service roads were closed to the public to protect wildlife—and the visitors. "You were on one that leads to a carcass dump site, where the park puts animals hit by cars. We placed a bison's remains there a week ago. Sometimes wolves and bears fight over the meat."

"Jade was seen nearby." Laura's heart raced.

He regarded her steadily. "Your dog is lucky if she went to the dump and is still alive. If you want to go there again, an armed ranger will have to accompany you."

"It's *that* dangerous?"

"I'm going to make sure it's locked right now." He spun on his heels and trotted toward one of the park vehicles.

She rewarded Laila with another treat. "I guess we're under armed guard from here on out." But, she thought with a shiver, Jade isn't.

When David and Angie returned to the car after a fruitless twenty minutes in the woods, he complained his throat was sore from yelling.

Laura said between gritted teeth, "Didn't you read the poster? Or hear the rangers?"

His face reddened. "That advice doesn't apply to me. Or Angie."

Laura drove in icy silence to the Canyon Lodge entrance.

David stayed in the car with a throbbing knee. This time, Laura was less sympathetic for his pain. As she checked them in, Laura saw another of Jade's flyers posted next to the desk. The young Aussie's blue eyes looked up at the camera, causing Laura's heart to ache with frustration. Tomorrow had to be better, she thought.

After tapping on some computer keys, the young woman said, "Welcome to Yellowstone. Enjoy your visit."

Laura filled out the requisite forms with shaky hands. "Thanks, but this isn't a vacation." She nodded toward the poster. "We're the ones who lost their dog."

"Oh." Her face softened in sympathy. "We tell everybody to keep an eye out for her." She tapped on her keyboard again. "I see Kat Brekken made your reservation. How long are you staying?"

"Until we get her." Laura swallowed hard. "Or Labor Day, whichever comes first."

That evening, as David, Laura, and Angie sat in the Canyon Lodge Restaurant, an outdoorsy woman with a cap of brown hair arrived. She scanned the dining room. A smile broke out on her face as she strode over to them.

"You must be Jade's family." She looked pointedly at David's braced leg balanced on a chair.

"Pleased to meet you, Kat." David started to get up.

"Stay put!" Kat patted his shoulder.

Laura stood and hugged the older woman. "We can't thank you enough for all you've done for us."

"We all appreciate it," Angie added.

"Not just me. There're at least a hundred people searching for her." Kat eased into one of the chairs.

David took a sip of beer. "I can't believe strangers put so much effort into the search."

Kat continued. "Yellowstone lost some of its magic this summer. We could all use some good news for a change."

Laura noticed Kat's expression, and wondered what had happened this season to cause her such sadness.

David frowned. "We missed Jade today by about ten minutes."

"If you hadn't stopped to take the picture of the bear, we might have been there on time." Angie toyed with her fries.

David glowered at his daughter. "Woulda, shoulda, coulda."

Laura shook her head. "When I saw you both running and shouting into the woods, my heart about stopped."

"I thought for sure she was there, staring at us," Angie explained to Kat. "I just knew she'd come to me."

David's color deepened. "All I could think was my pup was close after being gone for so long."

Kat shifted in her seat. "It's important that no one yells her name, or runs after her, not even her family."

Laura shot David an I-told-you-so-look.

"I just thought she was over the accident since she'd been seen so much lately." He twirled a napkin with his good hand.

Kat leaned forward. "You *must* not chase after her, David. Let her come to you."

Since Jade appeared to run from everyone, it was time, Laura thought, to offer her theory.

"Kat, what if you ask the volunteers to form a ring and herd Jade toward Canyon Village?"

Kat's eyes narrowed. "That might work. I'll have them start in the morning."

Chapter Seventeen

BEAR WARNINGS

THIRTY-EIGHT DAYS MISSING—Laila nuzzled Laura's hand, then gave it a lick. Laura opened one eye, glanced at the time, and groaned. Just once she'd like to sleep in, especially after the twelve-hour drive and disappointment yesterday. She yawned and pulled back the covers, trying not to disturb David. Angie rolled over in the other bed and bunched her pillow.

Laura threw on her hoodie and jeans, and led Laila into the cool morning air. The rosy eastern sky had Laura trying to recall the adage about the dawn's hue foretelling the fortune for the day. Frost steamed off the tall grasses in the meadow across from the service station.

Tourists walked in pairs studying maps. Many of them had dogs on leash. Occasionally they stopped and peered through binoculars. In a car parked at the edge of the service station, a man peered at the meadow. Good grief, she thought. It was early in the day for sightseeing.

Then she realized with a start that they were volunteers, combing the area for Jade.

The man in the car caught her gaze, and nodded a greeting.

She walked over to the open window and leaned in. "Are you looking for our dog?"

"I am." His face crinkled into a smile. "I'm Steve."

He appeared to be a man more comfortable in front of a computer screen, rather than in a dawn search and rescue operation. She shook his hand and introduced herself. "And they're volunteers also?"

"Most of them. So, you're the owner who came up with the plan." He said they had all arrived shortly before dawn to encircle Jade. He had volunteered to search while visiting his son, and was staying in the employee dorms with him.

"I had no real idea. I mean I knew lots of people were looking, but...." Her throat tightened. "We don't know how to thank you all for everything you're doing." Laila barked and placed her paws on the door, and Steve gave her head a pat.

"We just hope we find Jade soon."

"Me too. We just missed her yesterday." She turned away thinking they only had a week—at most—to find Jade.

An hour later, after a buffet breakfast where Laura stuffed her purse with crispy bacon, the family walked the meadow. They placed Jade's crate blanket and toys in what they hoped were strategic places.

"Let's go see the live traps. I want to visit my clothes," David joked.

They rounded the service station, and stopped at the empty spot where David's SUV had been towed after the accident.

"Your car was here, right Dad?" Angie scanned the parking lot.

He pointed to the space now covered in broken glass.

"It was right here. Kat thinks the scent might be what drew Jade to Canyon."

They walked to the edge of the lot where traps were covered in David's dew-soaked clothing, and redolent with strong-smelling dog food. Laila sniffed at the side of the cage.

Angie wrinkled her nose. "No wonder Jade hasn't gone into these. They're disgusting."

Laura pulled her Aussie away from the trap. "Well, Kat thinks the scent for a dog actually paints a picture in their memory."

Angie crossed her arms. "Some picture. Rags and rotten meat."

"At least the rangers set them." David gave his daughter a penetrating look. "They've gone to a lot of trouble."

Please don't argue again, thought Laura. Their bickering wasn't normal. The stress of losing Jade had worn on their usually good relationship. She decided to change the subject. "What do you think about going back to the service road?"

"Good idea." David limped away. "Let's go find Jade. We don't have time to waste."

Laura breathed a sigh. "Great. I'll call the rangers."

Patti Johnson arrived early Sunday afternoon at Canyon Village. Patti had met Kevin Torphy and his wife in Mammoth Hot Springs employee housing when he'd started working in the park early that year. After seeing his plea for help on Facebook, she finally had some time off from her job to help again. First, she called him to confirm the lost dog was still alive, and was surprised at his answer. With her life-long knowledge of Yellowstone, she'd figured Jade would last forty-eight hours maximum before she became prey.

As she got out of the car, she spotted Kevin in the service station parking lot along with Kat, who was speaking into a walkie-talkie.

"Check the perimeter."

A scratchy voice replied, "Negative to the south."

"Ten-four that."

As Patti approached, Kat greeted her. "Welcome back. You're carrying bear spray?"

Patti smiled and carefully patted the container on her belt. "You bet. It's hard to imagine the dog has survived this long."

Kat was emphatic. "Jade is alive and we *will* find her."

It was still difficult for Patti to believe, but she had to admit Kat was infectiously determined. "Where was she last seen?"

Kevin pointed toward the meadow. "There and behind the service station."

Patti decided to check out the woods first. As she hiked, the underbrush thickened and the light turned murky. A vole scampered across the forest floor, startling her. She wasn't trained in search and rescue, but she was an experienced hiker. She fingered her bear spray. In the past, Patti had tested her ability to remove the safety lever. It took her seven seconds, too long for a bear charge. Since then, she didn't go anywhere with the safety on.

Once after a hike she'd tossed her jacket into the back seat of her friend's Jeep. The unlocked bear spray in the pocket detonated, exploding its stinging contents throughout the confined space. Chagrined, she'd tied her windbreaker to the top of the SUV for the ride home. Multiple washings later, she'd been able to wear it again. She hadn't been invited to hike with that friend again.

She jumped at a rustle in the dappled woods. She removed the can from her pocket. In the swaying underbrush, something caught her eye. A shiver ran down her arm. Was that a dog or a bear?

More movement. She stopped, and held her breath. She thought she heard a growl. The hair on the back of her neck stood up. What was she supposed to do if it was the missing dog? Not call her name, turn her back, then what? She knew what to do if it was a bear. She raised the spray.

It was not black and white, but brown, with a large pink tongue hanging from its mouth while it panted. The dog wagged its tail.

A man appeared behind it, and Patti let out her breath with a *whoosh*. She recognized her coworker, George. "Are you looking for Jade?"

"Not now, but I was earlier—and I saw her! She shot past me like an arrow."

"So it's not a rumor."

"I almost caught her." He put two fingers an inch or so apart. "She was this close." He eyed the bear spray still in her hand. "Be careful with that stuff, will you?"

"And you be careful without it."

He gave her a rueful glance and set off with his dog.

Patti moved to the meadow. In the tall browning grass, a large yellow object caught her eye. She examined what appeared to be a kind of stuffed animal.

She made a face. The thing was filthy, and was a convoluted cross between a lollipop and an alien rabbit. Could it be Jade's? She'd never seen a dog play with the likes of this...toy. No, she decided. It must be a child's teething object. Perhaps a hiker carried a baby on his back and the kid threw it on the ground, unnoticed.

Well, she thought, you don't litter in Yellowstone National Park— not even a cigarette ash. She gingerly picked up the object with a Kleenex, resolving to throw it in a bin as soon as she had a chance.

Laura pulled in front of the chained entrance to the service road. A park vehicle squeezed in next to them, and an armed ranger jumped from it.

Through the open window, he said, "We'll be behind you. We'll leave some space so we don't scare your dog away." He eyed the interior of the car, where a loaded platter of bacon and cheese sat next to Angie. "I suppose you're trying to lure with that." He scanned the area. "Careful. You might get a bear interested too."

"And you have it next to *me*," Angie muttered.

Laura promised to be cautious, as she drove through the gate. The ranger followed, then locked it with a sturdy chain. Dense trees and four-foot berms flanked the exit. The road was a swathe cut through thick brush and woods. An unexpected sense of claustrophobia gripped Laura. They were locked in. Trapped. She knew she needed to shake it off. But, she admitted to herself, she was scared.

She tried to console herself. What could go wrong with armed rangers behind them?

Pine branches scraped the side of her car when she veered around potholes, and a cool breeze came in from the open car windows. David called and whistled for Jade when Laura stopped every few feet. The three of them peered into the thick underbrush.

"Is it my imagination, or is it darker than I remember?" Laura squinted through binoculars.

"It's straight out of a fairy tale," Angie said. "And not in a good way."

David looked skyward. "It's overcast, that's all."

"There're just as many bear warning signs as I remember," Angie added.

"Well, the rangers are right behind us, if we need them." Laura studied the rearview mirror and saw nothing but empty road.

Angie turned around. "Where?"

"They said they'd give us space. Don't worry," David assured her. "I'm sure they're not far away."

They rode for another half an hour, continuing to call for Jade. "Stop for a second. What's that?" David pointed to a post with a sheet affixed to it. Before anyone answered, he opened the car door and climbed out. "Only one way to see."

"I really don't think you should get out," Laura called after him.

"I don't like this." Angie sat wide-eyed, her head turning left and right.

Laura silently agreed with her. She inhaled the strong aromas of sharp cheddar and bacon. Perhaps they should roll up the windows.

David limped back to the car. "We must be near the carcass dump. There's a list of bison killed over the summer. The last one was hit by a car a week ago. I wonder how long it takes to strip one to the bone."

"Gross." Angie made a gagging noise. "Let's go, Laura."

After making a U-turn at the chained western entrance, they spotted the ranger vehicle driving toward them in the opposite direction.

"See? They were right behind us." David waved at them. "Only about half a mile or so."

"Only," Angie grumbled.

"Well, at least we didn't see Jade around here." Laura shuddered at the thought of blood-smeared predators lurking in the forest, feeding on carcasses.

They bounced along the road for a few more minutes, when David called out, "Stop the car!"

There was movement in the dense underbrush. Something in variegated hues moved through the trees. It was definitely an animal.

"It might be her!" David stepped out of the car. "J-a-ade! Here girl!"

The face that emerged was dark and without a trace of white on it. Then the rest of the grizzly appeared. It looked to be as colossal as the one they'd seen the day before.

"Get back in the car!" Laura's heart thumped as she rolled up the windows.

The bear charged toward them with a loud grunt.

Cursing aloud, David scrambled back into the vehicle as fast as his injuries allowed.

"Hurry up!" Laura watched the bear approaching. David slammed the car door. Angie screamed, and Laura stomped on the accelerator.

The grizzly wasn't giving up the chase. Through the plume of dust behind the car, Laura could make out the bear nearing the bumper. With gritted teeth, she drove over ruts that launched the SUV into the air. A stab of pain shot through her bruised ribs as the seatbelt dug in. David grunted and Laila's metal carrier rattled with each bone-rattling bounce.

Swerving around the potholes, her car tore through undergrowth while pine boughs scraped the roof.

Where were the rangers? Her eyes focused on the rearview mirror. She couldn't see anything but the bear running behind them.

Laura prayed she wouldn't get a flat tire as the accelerator inched toward forty miles an hour. The locked gate couldn't be far ahead.

Hadn't she seen a YouTube video of a bear breaking into a car by smashing the windows?

The gate was chained. There was no way to go off road. She might have to try to drive through it. She doubted it was even possible, but it appeared to be the only alternative.

Then, she checked her rearview mirror. The bear had disappeared.

She slowed the SUV, and found herself shaking with adrenaline. Angie and David let go of their handgrips. No one spoke for several minutes.

Finally, David broke the silence. "That was one pissed-off black bear."

Laura corrected him. "That was a grizzly."

"No it wasn't. It was a black bear."

"A. Black. Bear." Angie rubbed her temples.

A few minutes later, the rangers pulled in behind them.

"Any luck?"

"Not a sign of Jade. Just a bear," Laura replied.

"Not surprising. We detoured to check the carcass. It was stripped clean." He unlocked the chain and waved them through.

David turned to Laura. "I wonder if the bear was too late to the party to get anything."

She took a deep breath. "Let's hope Jade won't try for her share."

Laura obeyed the speed limits as she drove to Canyon Village, wondering if her plan to encircle Jade had worked. When they arrived, David winced with pain at every step. She found a chair for him, and suggested he sit in the meadow across from the service station.

"Remember Kat told us not to chase after her."

"Like I could." He picked at the surgical tape on his braced knee. The surgical staples had been removed the week before. He stared through his binoculars. "My pup will come to me, won't she?" Turning away from Laura, he wiped his eyes.

"I'm sure." Laura patted his arm. At least I hope she does, she added to herself. It was breaking her heart to see him so emotional.

Angie walked the meadow, gingerly carrying her bear spray, determined to stay out of the woods and in sight of civilization.

Laila tugged on her leash as Laura walked toward the employee dorms where Jade had been spotted. Laura stopped short and stared at a small sedan in one of the parking lots. In the passenger side window, a handwritten sign with an arrow pointing to a severely crushed right fender read, "YES IT WAS A BUFFALO! (HE WASN'T HURT.)"

Laura had to laugh.

The sun lowered in the sky. Laila barked as if to tell Laura to keep moving. Laura fed her the last piece of cheese, and took it as a sign to end the search for the day.

Laura walked to David, still sitting in his chair.

"Has the plan worked?" She bent and kissed his cheek.

He gave her a small smile. "Not yet, but I've met some nice folks searching for her. They're hopeful she'll come to me."

Angie ambled over from the direction of the woods, and pointed. "There are tons of volunteers around."

A woman in well-worn hiking gear approached them from across the meadow.

Patti introduced herself, and pointed toward the trees behind the service station. "Did you know your dog was seen there this morning?"

David shook his head. "No, I did not."

Laura's stomach knotted. Why did they ever leave the area? One wasted day—complete with a bear chase—and only six days left.

Patti pointed to a spot near the edge of the woods. "I found this filthy yellow thing in the meadow. It has long ears and a face. I thought it might be litter, like something a kid might teethe on and dropped it...but maybe?" She reached in her pocket and showed them.

"That's Tweety, Jade's favorite toy." David frowned. "Wait. You wanted to throw it out?"

"Sorry, sorry." Patti's face reddened. "I'll put it back where I found it. It just didn't look like a normal dog toy."

Patti headed toward the edge of the woods.

A bubble of mirth rose in Laura; she couldn't contain it any longer. She started a chuckle that grew into a full-on belly laugh.

Angie grinned. "You have to admit, it is weird-looking." With a wave, she walked away. "I'm going to get ready for dinner."

At first, David looked confused, but then he smiled.

There were tears on Laura's face.

"Filthy...yellow...thing." She managed to gasp out.

David laughed along with her. "Good enough to teethe on...."

"But not good enough for a dog!" She managed to blurt it out before another gale took over. "Oh God, it hurts when I do this." Her ribs ached, but she couldn't stop.

David rose from his chair and held a now tearful Laura. Laila barked, wagging her tail.

Finally, Laura took a few deep breaths. "I needed that. I haven't had such a good laugh in a long time." She had been about to add, "at least since the accident."

Then she realized it had been years ago, before her husband became so ill and she'd become his caregiver. There'd been so few laughs for so many years. "Eons, anyway."

She shakily pulled back from David's embrace. The moon rose on one horizon as the sun set on the other. "People will think we're crazy standing out here laughing in the meadow."

He wiped a tear from her cheek with his thumb, then kissed her lightly on the lips.

"Yeah. Crazy."

Chapter Eighteen

WAVING STEAK AND MEATBALLS

FORTY-TWO DAYS MISSING—Since they had failed to catch a glimpse of Jade as they drove around on Monday, David implemented a new plan. If he sat above the meadow, he reasoned he could spot Jade moving through the tall grass. After asking around, he discovered the highest point was a hill behind the Canyon Horse Corral.

Laura and Angie dropped him off at the riding stable, while they planned to comb the rest of the Canyon area. The sweet smell of horses, leather, and hay struck him as he limped to the wooden porch where a sign read:

CANYON 2 HOUR RIDE

This ride leaves the corral, heading into timber and crossing a large meadow. A short stretch of our ride traverses through an area of forest regrowth following the legendary 1988 Yellowstone Fire. The ride continues along the rim of the Cascade Canyon through which Cascade Creek flows. A nice view into the canyon is possible from Coyote Slide. The ride returns to the corral through a series of meadows.

He noted nearby Cascade Creek was a likely source of water for Jade. What he hadn't seen, however, were any posters of his missing dog. Riders would be in a perfect position to see Jade along the off-road trail. Puzzled, he went into the office and introduced himself.

A young cowboy greeted him with a smile, and nodded at the metallic brace on David's leg. "The ride might be a bit rough on you." He glanced at the purple cast on his hand. "And one-handed too."

"I'm not here for a trail ride." David explained his plan, and was shocked that the cowboy didn't know anything about Jade. He pulled a flyer from his backpack. "Do you mind if I hang up a couple of these?"

"Not at all. We'll tell the riders and keep an eye out for your little doggie."

David limped to the top of the nearby hill. Pulling his binoculars from the case, he studied the topography in a mile or so radius. Below him, woods outlined the meadow, and the creek meandered, a silver ribbon of light. He could make out the service road, the Canyon Village Lodge, employee dorms, and the service station. From above, the beauty of the place overtook him. It all looked so serene, yet he knew firsthand how wild and untamed it was.

Interrupting his surveillance, a woman hiked toward him carrying a camera and lens he reckoned cost as much as his SUV. Introducing herself, she pointed up at the sky. A red-tailed hawk circled aloft on the warm thermals of air.

She pointed skyward. "This is the kind of thing I'm after."

David explained he was searching for his lost pup.

The woman had heard of Jade. "I've been keeping an eye out for your dog."

Hours passed as he scanned the meadow, searching for any movement that might signal Jade. In the nearby thicket, a tumbling series of whistles sounded: *sweet, sweet, I'm so sweet.* The hawk swooped low and a flock of tiny yellow birds emerged, chasing the raptor, creating a cacophony of sound.

David allowed himself to be distracted for a moment. He turned his attention to the warblers in a life and death struggle, cloaked in beauty. How many birdsongs, melodic to humans' ears, he thought, are cries of desperation and longing?

The hawk cleared the horizon and was replaced by a raven circling above. The woman put her camera down.

"How unusual. Ravens usually stay down on the meadow, near the people." She adjusted her camera settings and reviewed photos. "Or near the wolves." She explained the symbiotic relationship between the birds and the predators. "They're remarkably intelligent."

"Really? I thought they were just scavengers."

"They're adaptive. But doesn't that make them smart?"

He considered her remark. Adjusting to one's environment and surviving—his father, the scientist, would've approved. Jade too had somehow adapted to the wild.

The next day, the trio decided to take a different tack: follow Kat's advice and stay put in the meadow, letting their scent carry. David rested on his lawn chair, taking in the reactions of the people at the nearby service station.

Laura's parked SUV was festooned with David's colorful briefs and Angie's Victoria's Secret lacy underwear that spilled from the open windows. Most people pumping gas gave the vehicle a double take. A few of them with perplexed expressions walked over to it.

They also might wonder at the strange setup in the meadow with lawn chairs, Jade's crate blanket, dog food, toys, and water bowls strewn about. They would, he figured, appear to be having some type of bizarre picnic across from a uniquely decorated SUV.

A pair of women ambled toward him with a dog on a leash. As they neared, he recognized Patti.

"This is my friend, Paula. I put Tweety back in the spot I found it." Patti nodded toward the car where a breeze lifted the edge of a lacy camisole. "Yours, I take it?"

"Not the girlie things. I'm here letting my 'scent carry.'" Eager to change the subject, he noticed she carried two baggies. "What do you have there?"

She laughed. "Everything I could find in my refrigerator. Leftover steak." She lifted the other bag. "And some Italian meatballs."

David smiled at her. "It just might work."

"Well, we'll leave you to share your masculine scent." Patti and her friend ambled off with their dog. He heard them laughing and calling out, "Here puppy, puppy!" while waving the meat in the air. He tried to remember if Jade had ever had a meatball, but under the circumstances, she'd probably eat anything.

He, Laura, and Angie spent the morning strategically placing themselves around the area with the precision of a drill team. Angie moved her chair and set it diagonally across from her father. Laura relocated to another corner where David could hear Laila barking. He wondered if the puppy was gaining weight after so many helpings of bacon and cheese.

Around noon, Laura strolled toward him, Laila tugging on the lead. "It's lunchtime. I'm hungry and thirsty."

David laughed. "No doubt." He grabbed Laila's leash and watched Laura walk toward the store. Laura was unabashed in her love of food and wine. How she managed to stay so slim remained a mystery to him. Not that he minded. Men's heads turned when the tall, leggy woman with a sunny smile walked by. She had been so kind to him over the last few weeks, he constantly marveled at his luck finding her on the internet dating service.

It had been, he realized, all because of Jade. They'd connected with their love of Aussies. Had it not been for losing his pup, they might never have been together for the last six weeks.

Laura came back carrying several large bags. "A meal without wine is called breakfast." She expertly uncorked the bottle of Chardonnay, and poured each of them a plastic glassful. She sat on Jade's blanket and assembled cheese and lunchmeats on the crackers.

"You know, I wonder how Jade has managed with the wolves." Angie chewed on a cracker. "I would think she's been close to them."

"She probably scared the crap out of them with those blue eyes," David joked.

Laura laughed and handed him a loaded cracker. "They probably think she's some kind of spirit ghost come to haunt them."

David peered into the woods. "You know, I get the funniest feeling she's watching us."

Angie shivered. The wind had picked up, lifting the corner of Jade's blanket. "You think?"

"She always was one independent pup." David's dimples showed above his salt and pepper goatee.

"She must be hungry." Laura pointed at a vole sniffing only a few feet away. "These look like pretty easy prey." Laila ignored the rodent while chewing on salami. "I talked to Steve the volunteer this morning. He goes out in the middle of the night to check for Jade. He thinks she's lapping up the ice cream that kids dropped from their cones. Or eating popcorn spilled on the ground."

"That's possible." David looked toward the flock of ravens that had gathered in the sapling near them. They seemed to be waiting for any food morsels the group might leave. One of them flew off toward an open trash container.

"I know the Park Service is strict about garbage, but you never know."

"Dad...she'll starve this winter with the tourists gone. I can't leave her here."

Laura gathered up the remainder of their lunch and took Laila's leash. "I could use a cup of coffee. Walk with me?"

Angie opened her mouth as if to say something, then nodded.

David looked away. He could've ended the several-day-long argument Laura had just thwarted. He was just too damn Texas-proud. Men had obligations, and despite his liberal leanings, some values didn't change. One of the cornerstones firmly implanted in his psyche nagged at him. Men were supposed to support and protect their loved ones and family.

He couldn't adhere to the dictum if he wasn't working. The company he owned needed him. He was critical to the operation, everything from making sales, designing the advertising, to collecting money.

Employees depended on him for their livelihoods, including people living in homeless shelters who counted on their paychecks for hanging his company's advertising on front doors.

Additionally, he still provided for Angie, who was working her way up the beauty salon hierarchy. Neither of them could afford to stay indefinitely in Yellowstone's lodging, and she needed to return to work. If he left before they found Jade, it might drive a permanent wedge between him and the daughter he loved.

Then there was beautiful Laura, the kind, fun woman who'd been forced into becoming his caregiver before she'd even been certain she was his "girlfriend." He admired her gumption at becoming an agility judge, using her interests and passion to resume earning a living.

She had left her profession to take care of her husband's rapidly deteriorating health. Once he was institutionalized, she tried getting back into the same sales and management career. She'd faced the unspoken prejudice of age and being out of that sector for too many years. Many jobs were going to younger people comfortable with current technology and willing to work for less money as they started their working lives.

He knew she had been accustomed to the finer things in life before her husband had taken ill. She spoke of travel, restaurants, Champagne. She was the kind of woman who deserved the best, but never complained. It killed him to watch her fight for composure whenever she suggested they go out for dinner, and he countered with cooking in. What kind of relationship could he offer her if his business suffered?

Too many people depended on him. No. It was not an option. He had to get back to his business, with or without Jade, even if it meant a rift with his daughter.

The wind in the meadow picked up in earnest, sending a chill down David's bare legs below his cargo shorts. He wondered where Laura and Angie were. They should've returned by now.

The brown grass rustled and a single raven flew overhead, reminding him of yesterday's conversation with the photographer. The scent of drying leaves foreshadowed the upcoming winter. David needed to stand up, his leg caught in a ferocious cramp. He stretched, then hobbled up a small rise and whistled for Jade.

Everything went into slow motion. He was vaguely aware of the sound of Angie and Laura's voices. They must be back, he thought.

A black and white head popped up from behind a log, fifty yards from him.

He locked eyes with his dog, reading panic instead of recognition. "Jade!"

He heard Angie and Laura's calls as they sprinted toward him.

"There she is! There she is!" He pointed at the log. Before he could move, Jade took off at a dead run, zig zagging away into the woods.

Laura and Angie stood next to him, panting from their run.

David pointed with a shaky hand. "She was right there! I don't know who was more startled—me or her." His heart pounded as he examined where she had appeared. The grass was trampled down, like where a deer might bed. They searched the meadow, finding several more likely spots.

He was shocked. "She's been sleeping out here, not in the woods like we thought."

"At least you saw her!" Laura examined the trampled grass.

"Jade's still alive, Dad." Angie's voice quivered with emotion.

Yes, she was alive. His world spun in a kaleidoscope of emotion. In the background, he heard volunteers calling for her. All of the time spent searching for her, all of these people giving of themselves, all of the agony he was now going through. It was as useless as waving steak and meatballs in the air if Jade refused to come to him.

Stunned at the realization, he couldn't control his shaking hands. Waves of grief coursed through him, reminding him once more of his last great loss. He pictured his Australian shepherd Ozzy riddled with cancer.

"Are you sure?" the vet had asked. "There's no turning back once I begin."

Ozzy weakly lifted his head from the metal table and looked up at him.

David wanted to cling to his old friend, the one who spent every day with him for ten years. "Is he in pain?"

The vet looked at him kindly. "Probably."

He closed his eyes briefly. "Then yes. I am sure."

The vet administered one shot in the scruff of the dog's neck. Ozzy quieted, locking eyes with David.

"You're a good dog. The best."

Tears rolled down David's face as the vet injected Ozzy with the final drug. David had watched the light leave his companion's soft eyes and go dull. The one being who loved him unconditionally was gone. The grief had been almost unbearable. He was still recovering from it when his kids had bought Jade for him as a Father's Day present.

There would be no such gift of compassion to give Jade. This winter, his pup would starve if she wouldn't come to anyone. Overcome, he realized she was still alive, but no longer his dog.

His Jade wouldn't run from him.

His Jade was truly lost.

Chapter Nineteen

BRING JADE HOME

"The ethical and moral progress of any civilization
can be measured in how it treats its animals."
—Ghandi

FORTY-THREE DAYS MISSING—"I don't see the point in staying." David sat in the lawn chair, his braced leg extended. "It's costing a fortune every day we're here."

He stared dejectedly at the meadow. Laura knew he had slept poorly the night before since any hope had been extinguished. Jade's lack of recognition had broken his heart.

Angie bit her lip.

Laura reminded him, "Remember we're meeting Kat at the Roosevelt Lodge tonight? You wanted to see it."

She read a flicker of interest on his face at the mention of the historic area. He watched the History Channel at every opportunity. "Besides, at least we owe her dinner for all she's done for us." She was trying to buy them as much time as she could before he gave up and returned to Denver.

Angie blinked back tears.

When David didn't respond, Laura grabbed Laila's leash. "I'll go look for Jade in the meantime."

The wind rustled the drying leaves as she and her dog moved through the grass. She pondered David's theory that Jade slept in the tramped-down beds of grass. She had Laila sniff each one they discovered.

"Find Jade, girl!" Laila wagged her tail, then barked waiting for a treat. Laura sighed. Her Aussie was no bloodhound. At least Laila could bark, and that she did well.

Laura patrolled the edge of the woods. A mouse ventured within a foot of Laila, who took no notice of it. Perhaps Jade could make short work of catching the prey. She remembered her shock the first time, when on a long hike in Colorado, Jade had deposited an animal skull at Laura's feet. Afterward, she and David became accustomed to the animal parts Jade retrieved, including a large half-frozen deer leg.

Her hunting couldn't have been that successful in Yellowstone. David told them Jade was so thin that her ribs showed. She must be desperate for food, even starving.

Laura was puzzled as to why Jade ran from David. He must represent food, shelter, safety, and love to her. The shock of the accident should've lessened by now. She could only guess that the young Aussie had suffered additional traumas. Perhaps Jade had been pursued by packs of coyotes, or wolves. Laura knew firsthand the terror of a bear chase—and she had been inside the safe metal shell of a car.

The only thing Laura could conclude, was Jade's wild nature had taken over. In order to survive, she was no longer domesticated.

Jade had gone feral.

Laura returned with food and wine for another picnic lunch. David barely touched his food, but steadily sipped the Chardonnay.

"You'd better eat something." Laura nodded toward the sandwich balanced in his lap. "Keep up your strength and all." She attempted a weak smile.

He snorted. "Right. Like Jade will come to me and I'll have to grab her."

"She might." Laura decided now was not the time to discuss her new worries about Jade's behavior. "Keep some cheese around you too. You said she was thin. She must be hungry."

"Hungry? Starved is more like it."

"You need to stay positive."

He closed his eyes briefly. "You don't know what it's like to see someone you love, and they don't recognize you."

The blood throbbed in her temples and after an agonizing pause, she managed, "Actually, I do." Her eyes flooded with tears. As she stood, her lunch fell to the ground, knocking over her wine glass. "I need a break." Grabbing Laila's leash, they took off first at a jog, and then a full run. She ignored David's and Angie's calls.

Laila ran next to her, panting with her tongue lolling. Laura found herself heading south, toward the Grand Canyon of the Yellowstone, once her favorite place in the park.

She slowed to a walk on the crowded trail to the canyon. Around a bend, she came upon its vast expanse: rocks varnished in shades of red, yellow, and magenta as if a landscape painter had taken a brush to them. The Yellowstone River roared below, sending up a spume the sun caught in a rainbow. The nearby benches were crowded with tourists. She hiked along the steep rim until she found a boulder to rest on, set back from the canyon. Laila sank to the ground and rested her head on her paws.

Laura remembered the first time she'd been in the park, at five years of age. She'd saved a faded color photo of herself in front of the canyon. Just before the accident, she had David take a picture of her in the same pose for Throwback Thursday on Facebook. But she hadn't posted it. With Jade gone, anything reminding her of the vacation had only stung.

How innocent she and David had been before the accident. Neither of them suspected everything would change in a few short seconds.

However, Laura ached today for a different time in Yellowstone. In 2012, she'd brought her husband for a trip, along with their Golden Retriever, Wiki, hoping that a change of scenery would benefit them both. Quinn, in the throes of dementia and unable to drive, had enjoyed the car ride.

They sat glorying in the view of this canyon. She had measured his every reaction, thrilling at the slightest pleasure registering on his countenance. He stared, engrossed in the spectacle as if it were being unveiled to him for the first time, even though they returned day after day. Wiki, his heart dog, sat close by his side, occasionally nuzzling his hand.

It had been a bittersweet last trip together. His doctor found a lump on Quinn's breast. Her husband carried the BRCA 1 gene inherited from his mother who died in her early thirties of ovarian cancer. Laura became his caretaker as he had a mastectomy and radiation treatments afterward. All the while, he remained confused and disoriented.

Not long afterward, her husband had lost all ability to speak. Once, he wandered from his institution and was found blocks away. Formerly a kind, gentle man, he recently had turned violent, assaulting other patients. When Laura visited, he was agitated and didn't acknowledge her or his dog.

David's comment today had pierced her heart.

The man she married twenty-six years ago, the person she loved so much, had no idea who she was.

She tried to hide her face from curious tourists. Laila wiggled onto her lap and licked her tears. Hugging her dog tightly, she sobbed into her fur. Laila's tail wagged and she yipped a greeting. Swiping her eyes, Laura glanced up and saw David.

"How...how did you find me?" she sniffed.

He sat heavily on the ground next to her. "You're easier to locate than my dog, that's for sure." Laila licked his face, and he gave her a pat on the head. "Angie knew this was your favorite place. She left your car in the lot over there." He reached for Laura with his good hand. "I am so sorry. I didn't think."

She moved to the grass next to David and leaned in, ignoring the sideways glances of passing tourists. He knew about Quinn and had been supportive. But she never discussed some emotions with anyone, including David.

"I came here with Quinn. It was one of our last good times together." A waterfall of guilt washed over her. She was still technically married, and their wedding anniversary was exactly twenty days in the future. "Sometimes I wonder if the accident was a sort of cosmic punishment for starting our new relationship."

"I don't believe that. You've been so good to Quinn. If anything, you should be admired."

"If only I had turned faster, moved away sooner when I saw that truck in our lane..." She drew in a breath.

"No, no, it was just bad luck. Two minutes earlier or later at that point in the road and it wouldn't have happened."

"Now your knee may never be the same...Jade is gone. We may not find her."

He patted her hand. "Maybe I should have had a stronger carrier. We can second-guess everything. What matters is how we go forward."

"Even if we don't find Jade?"

He reached over and hugged her. "Even if."

She took a deep breath. "Kat's always saying Yellowstone needs some good news. I could use some too."

"I know, sweetheart. I know."

The trio arrived at the Roosevelt Lodge before Kat. The long, rustic log structure sat in an idyllic setting, surrounded by quaking aspen trees. A sagebrush meadow in the foreground was set off by blue mountains lining the horizon. Small log cabins dotted the surrounding area.

The three of them sat on the porch with brochures, but none of them were really reading, Laura realized. Under other circumstances, David would have been thrilled to learn more about the historic former campground.

Strangely, none of the lodges in Yellowstone had rooms in the building; they were established as eating and socializing centers.

A black pickup truck pulled in, and Kat emerged. "Welcome to Roosie!" After hugs, Kat led them into the dining room. Stone fireplaces flanked the room that bustled with activity.

"This is my favorite place to eat in the park. They named it for Theodore Roosevelt, since he loved to camp near here."

Laura smiled. "This is gorgeous." The warm log walls and burnished hardwood floors glistened.

"Teddy was interesting. He was an avid trophy hunter, but he was also a conservationist. Without him, there might not be a Yellowstone National Park."

"I'm a history buff myself," David offered. They discussed the continuing battle to protect the environment and the wildlife both in the national parks and the surrounding areas.

After their food arrived, Kat broached the subject. "Let's talk about Jade running from David."

David picked at his fries.

At his dejected expression, Laura asked, "It's great he saw Jade, right? I mean, she was about fifty yards away. She looked right at him, answering his whistle."

It certainly wasn't the time to voice her own theory that Jade wouldn't be coming to anyone any time soon.

Angie set her water down. "It's encouraging, right Kat?"

"She may just need some more time to adjust." Kat regarded their three long faces. "This was just the first time you came close to her. She might not have caught your scent very well from that distance."

"Maybe not." David sounded unconvinced.

"And you might have startled her, and sent her running. The next time she might not be so surprised."

"Yes, Dad. Maybe you just surprised her." Angie wore a hopeful expression.

Kat still sounded upbeat. "This might encourage you. Sandy Monville, who I met this year at the *Speak for Wolves Conference*, set this up today." She went on to explain a new Facebook page that would consolidate all information on the progress of the search. "It's called *Bring Jade Home*. Check it out." She pushed her phone toward them.

Laura smiled. "That's great news."

"Sandy also set up a GoFundMe page, to help you with expenses."

David blinked several times. "I can't accept charity."

"Spoken like a true male. We'll need your particulars."

He shrugged. "Sure."

Laura nodded toward Kat. "I'll get them for you."

When the bill for dinner arrived, David grabbed it. He opened his wallet, slid one credit card out a bit, put it back, and selected another. In that moment, Laura realized the money from GoFundMe, whatever it amounted to, was like sticking a finger in a financial dike about to burst if David didn't get back to running his business.

They walked into the cold night. Above them, stars glittered in the dark firmament. After saying their goodbyes to Kat, Angie and David walked ahead.

Laura held back and hugged Kat tightly. "Thank you for every-thing." She saw her friend's puzzled expression in the dim light. "David has to go home soon. Believe me, he has no choice."

"Even without Jade?"

"I'm afraid so." Laura was helpless to add anything but another hug.

"That would be a shame. I know if you sit in the meadow, let your scent carry, and don't chase her, she will come to her family."

A cloud of sadness enveloped Laura. After all of the effort Kat and hundreds of others had made to find Jade, they might have to leave before the Aussie came to them.

Kat was insistent. "Promise me you won't give up. She's so close. I have this feeling. Just keep your dog barking by feeding her treats. I know Jade is hungry."

Laura agreed to do her best to convince David to stay until the last possible moment. As she walked to her car, she heard Kat's old pickup truck attempting to start, then finally catch. David and Angie were waiting for her in the SUV, where she found them both swiping their eyes. Laura didn't need to ask. She understood why David had turned away from her.

David must have told Angie to pack. They were leaving tomorrow.

Chapter Twenty

"IS THAT A DOG OR A DEER?"

FRIDAY, SEPTEMBER 4: FORTY-FOUR DAYS MISSING—"Oh Laila, not yet."
Laura rolled over and glanced at her phone. It was only a little after
seven. Her Aussie licked her hand, then ran toward the door and back.
Laura knew she'd better take her dog out before she woke everyone
else. David rolled over, turning his back to her. Angie curled into a
fetal position with the pillow over her head.

Laura had felt David tossing and turning much of the night. They'd
had a whispered conversation around three in the morning. He had
admitted he needed to go home, not only to run his business but for his
own mental health. "I dread spending one more day in that meadow."

Yet David was torn, still holding onto a slim hope of recovering Jade if he stayed until Labor Day. He whispered he would delay
making the decision until he had a chance to sleep on it.

Laura wasn't optimistic about what his choice would be. He'd
suffered enough heartbreak. Jade's lack of recognition had been the
final affront.

She dressed and let Laila pull her out of the cabin. Behind them, an elk bugled, its eerie sound muted by the surrounding fog. It was the first time she'd ever heard its plaintive call for dominance, sending goosebumps down her arms. It was the fall mating season, reminding her winter wasn't far behind.

Mist covered Canyon Village as the sun illuminated the eastern horizon. In the hazy dawn, a few pairs of tourists were scattered about. Laura didn't recognize any volunteers. Then, she spotted a familiar sight, and strode to a truck positioned at the service station.

"Have you been here long, Steve?"

"On and off all night. I thought she might come out to feed in the dark." He glanced toward the meadow. "It's a beautiful morning, isn't it?"

Laura agreed as Laila placed her paws on the window. Steve gave the puppy her usual pat on the head.

"Well, now that you're here, I think I'll drive over to the other end of the field. That way we'll cover more area."

He'd been so devoted to the cause; Laura didn't have the heart to tell him this was most likely the last morning she'd be helping with any surveillance. Laila yanked on her leash. "I'd better walk her."

"Call me if you see Jade." Steve started the engine. A couple of days before, they'd exchanged phone numbers. Everyone had been optimistic before Jade had run from David.

"You too." She watched him drive a few hundred yards away and park his car. Laila led her down through a small ditch, a few feet into the grass.

The fog had settled in the meadow. Wisps of steam rose up in the early morning light. Yellowstone was stunning, she thought, swallowing hard at the bitter realization she may never return to enjoy its beauty.

Laila tugged her toward a couple of tourists taking pictures. Laura had to pull her back from jumping on them. She hated to interrupt the photographers, but Laila already had.

"Gorgeous view, isn't it?"

They both smiled and the woman responded, "Yes, it certainly is."

Laura recognized their accent. "Are you British?"

The woman answered in the affirmative, and then added, "We're here at Yellowstone on holiday. And you?"

"From Denver, Colorado. And not exactly on vacation." She explained their dog, Jade, had been missing for over six weeks.

"And you think she's still alive. That's a miracle." The woman lifted her binoculars to scan the horizon. Laura decided to pretend she too was capturing memories, enjoying the splendid scenery instead of aching for the losses in her life.

As the sun grew stronger, the fog lifted, creating pockets of blue sky. Laura felt the warmth on her arms, promising another balmy day. She glanced at her phone. It was time to get back. If David decided to leave this morning, she had a long day of driving ahead.

She turned toward the cabin and hesitated. Out of the corner of her eye, she saw a raven circling over the meadow. It was a dark marker against the brilliant Rocky Mountain sky.

Beneath the black bird, about two hundred yards away, a murky shape moved away in the tall grass.

Her stomach somersaulted. Something in the coloring and form was familiar. She turned back to the couple, pointing toward the meadow. "See there? Is that a dog or a deer?"

The woman studied the movement through her binoculars.

Laura held her breath, waiting for the answer.

"It's definitely a dog."

With shaking hands, Laura phoned Steve. "I think I saw Jade, but she's heading south."

Wishing her the best of luck, the couple said, "We'll get out of your way."

Laura reached into her pocket and found treats left over from the day before. Laila barked.

"Want a treat? Want a treat?" She gave Laila cheese and bacon when her dog barked on cue. Laura hoped Laila's bark was distinctive enough to tell Jade that food was at hand.

She was vaguely aware of the sound of a car in the distance. Then, there was only Laila barking. Laura called for Jade, her voice high-pitched with excitement. "Here puppy, puppy. Here puppy, puppy."

Long minute after minute passed. Nothing. In a panic she called out, "Please Jade, don't run away again. Please!"

Tears stung her eyes. Doubt seeped in. It was useless. Why would Jade come to *her*?

Then Laura steadied herself and reached deep inside. She called on her years of dog training, which had given her patience, trust, and belief in her dogs and herself. She could do this.

In a small copse of trees fifty feet in front of her, Laura thought she saw a shrub quiver. Could it be? Had Jade circled the meadow, and was now hidden in the thicket?

Years of self-discipline helped her to stand firm, rooted to the ground.

With new urgency, she cajoled Laila to bark, and continued her chant calling for Jade.

A black and white face peered out of the trees.

Tears streamed down Laura's face. She was almost out of treats. "Please keep barking, Laila, please." Her hands shook as she gave her dog the last piece of cheese.

She held her breath. More of Jade emerged from the brush. Visualizing Jade home safe in David's arms, she believed it possible.

"Here puppy, puppy." She could barely speak as her heart pounded.

Then Jade, wearing her smile of greeting, raced through the yellowing grass directly to Laura.

Laura dropped on her knees, and Jade leapt on her, kissing her legs, her arms, her face. Laura hugged Jade's thin body, tears running down her cheeks. "Oh puppy, you're here, you're here." She prayed she was awake and this surreal scene wasn't a dream. Another lick to her face convinced her that the pup truly was in her arms after forty-four days, as if Jade had been waiting for this exact moment to be reunited.

Laila started a low growl, shaking Laura from her bliss. Her dog wasn't welcoming her former friend back any time soon. She was astonished the blue collar still hung loosely around Jade's neck. Laura grabbed it, along with a handful of fur, just in case.

Adrenaline tremors ran through Laura. Now, she had to keep the dogs apart, and not lose either of them. She was terrified her elation could turn to disaster if she lost her grip on Jade. Laila treated her former playmate like a stranger. Laura's mind raced. The tourists had moved out of sight.

Then she heard someone behind her. Steve approached with an open can of Spam, which he set in front of Jade. She devoured it in huge gulps.

"I only have the one leash. I never thought...." Laura held Laila at arm's length.

"No problem." He bent and removed the shoelaces from each of his hiking boots. He tied them together, and fastened the makeshift leash to Laila. Relieved, she looped Laila's lead lariat style around Jade's neck, not trusting the loose blue collar.

Steve led the growling Laila away. "I'll take her in my car and follow you."

Grasping the leash tightly, Laura ran her hands gently over the Aussie's thin body. Other than Jade's obvious weight loss, nothing appeared out of the ordinary, with the exception of a small scab on her upper lip.

"You don't even have a burr, girl."

Jade gave her a huge doggy kiss.

Laura shakily stood, and took the can of Spam away from Jade. "You can't have all of this at once, girl. You'll get sick." The absurdity of it was laughable. Jade had probably survived much worse.

As they walked along the road toward the cabin, Laura continued to feed Jade more Spam. At one point, Jade stopped and squatted.

Laura stared in dismay at the pile in the middle of the road. Feeding Jade must have triggered it.

Steve jumped from the car and ran toward her. "I'll clean it up, don't worry."

She regarded the plastic bag in his hand and smiled. "Were you a Boy Scout, Steve?"

He grinned. "Eagle Scout. By the way, I've called the rangers and let them know you have her."

Jade's news is traveling as fast as a Yellowstone wildfire, she thought. People stopped her. "Is that the missing dog?"

"It is!" Laura beamed and could barely take her eyes off Jade.

As they neared the employee dorms, people spilled out of doorways, cheering and calling out, "You found Jade!"

As the Aussie proudly paraded next to her, Laura felt like a handler who had just won Best in Show at Westminster. Laura visualized Jade nodding toward the judges, as if the attention was her due.

Outside of Canyon Lodge, a small crowd had gathered. Laura recognized some of the receptionists, who cheered and waved Jade's flyers with "FOUND" written across them.

The scene blurred through Laura's tears of joy. With every step, her burden of guilt lifted. Gratitude replaced sadness, relief replaced disappointment, hope replaced fear. It was true. They had Jade. David could bring her home.

Someone started to clap, and then applause broke out. Lifting her face toward the sun, Laura felt the warmth of pure unmitigated joy. Good news had finally come to Yellowstone—and to Laura.

Chapter Twenty-one

ONLY THE STRONG
SURVIVE YELLOWSTONE

"The strongest people find the courage and caring to help others,
even if they are going through their own storm."
— Roy T. Bennett, The Light in the Heart

FORTY-FOUR DAYS MISSING—David was in the middle of a vivid dream. In it, he heard the door unlock and Laura's bright voice ask, "Who's ready to see Jade?"

"Stop kidding around, Laura." David rolled over on the bed. Then he realized he'd spoken aloud. There was something in her tone. Laura wasn't the type to make cruel jokes.

He forced his eyes open as a black and white blur ran toward Angie.

"Oh my God, oh my God," Angie screamed as Jade lunged onto her bed and kissed her.

It took him a few seconds to take in the reality. He managed to choke out, "Jade."

189

Chapter Twenty-one

ONLY THE STRONG
SURVIVE YELLOWSTONE

"The strongest people find the courage and caring to help others,
even if they are going through their own storm."
— Roy T. Bennett, The Light in the Heart

FORTY-FOUR DAYS MISSING—David was in the middle of a vivid dream. In it, he heard the door unlock and Laura's bright voice ask, "Who's ready to see Jade?"

"Stop kidding around, Laura." David rolled over on the bed. Then he realized he'd spoken aloud. There was something in her tone. Laura wasn't the type to make cruel jokes.

He forced his eyes open as a black and white blur ran toward Angie.

"Oh my God, oh my God," Angie screamed as Jade lunged onto her bed and kissed her.

It took him a few seconds to take in the reality. He managed to choke out, "Jade."

Her blue eyes locked with his; his world shifted and spun as he studied the expression on her face. She tilted her head, as if to assess him.

Then, she smiled.

His dog leapt across the beds and landed next to David. He hugged her thin body to him as she licked his face.

"Jade." So many times, he'd called this single name over the last six weeks until he'd become hoarse. He buried his head in her fur, feeling her warmth and beating heart. This wasn't a dream. Her rear end quivered back and forth in a frenzy of excitement. He wiped his eyes with trembling hands and looked into her steady blue gaze.

Jade was real, and she was in his arms. He couldn't believe it.

He became aware of Laura standing next to him wearing a huge grin, the happiest expression he'd seen on her face since the accident. He gaped up at her in disbelief.

Angie jumped from her bed and sat next to him. Jade alternated between licking both of them.

"How?" He couldn't even form the words to ask. He was still in a state of shock.

"It was one of the best moments of my life." Laura knelt next to him with a blissful expression on her face, and told him every detail of how Jade came to her in the meadow.

"I think she recognized her buddy barking for treats." David suspected Laura was modestly downplaying her role. "Speaking of Laila, I have to get her and give Steve back his shoelaces. And I'm going to make a Champagne run."

With that, Laura gathered up an extra leash and more treats. "Don't feed Jade too much at once. She could get sick."

He nodded, and waited until she closed the door. Tearing himself away from Jade, he grabbed the rest of the Spam, opened a can of dog food, and poured it all in a bowl. Jade leapt from the bed and quickly gulped it down.

Angie giggled. "I'll get some cheese for her."

With Laila in tow, Laura returned balancing a variety of shopping bags. Jade wore an expression of pure contentment, her head on Angie's lap. Laila ignored her former buddy.

"What's wrong with your dog?" Angie asked. "I thought they were friends."

Laura shrugged. "I think she's a little mad at Jade for causing us all so much grief for six weeks."

Sometimes, David thought, a simple rational explanation sufficed. "Or maybe Jade just smells different, like a wild animal."

Laura set a few bags down. "It's possible. Steve thinks her last meal was buffalo poop."

"Wow." Angie frowned at Jade.

Laura laughed. "You may want to consider that the next time she kisses your face. I invited Steve to stop by tonight to celebrate, but he declined. He said witnessing Jade coming in was enough. I also suspect he's going to get some sleep. He was up most of last night searching for her, bless him." She handed one of her packages to David.

He took out a t-shirt with a bear's paw print in the middle and *Only the Strong Survive Yellowstone* imprinted on it. "Thank you. We need a matching one for Jade with *her* paw print."

At hearing David say her name, the Aussie's ears perked up and her rear waggled a bit. Then she set her head back down and closed her eyes.

Angie played with Jade's worn blue collar hanging loose on her neck. "Or have a kerchief made up with the saying. Would you like that, girl?" Jade turned and licked her hand.

Laura scanned the cabin. "You didn't overfeed her, did you?"

David tried to assume an innocent expression. "Of course not."

He and Angie exchanged brief grins behind Laura's back as she studied the empty cans in the garbage.

Laura spun around and gave both of them mock stern looks. "Why don't I believe you two?"

Angie and David shrugged, fighting back laughter. Jade was back and all was forgiven.

As soon as Laura could contact Kat, they arranged to meet at the Mammoth Hot Springs Hotel where a reporter would also join them. Kat was jubilant she didn't have to wait until she was off work to meet the dog whose rescue had inspired her for weeks.

David gazed out the car window with Jade on his lap. Laura wisely hadn't tried to convince him to put Jade in a crate for the hour and a half trip. The Grand Loop Road snaked through the mountains through the tight curves of the Dunraven Pass switchbacks. Laura, he noticed, wasn't clutching the steering wheel with white-knuckled intensity as she had ever since the accident. The sun sparkled on Antelope Creek, and eventually they drove along the roaring Yellowstone River.

"I could come back here now." David ran his hand over Jade, who alertly stared out the window. He wondered what she thought as the wilderness flashed by.

Laura smiled. "Me too."

As soon as they arrived, Kat and her officemates ran outside to greet them.

"This was stuck on my cubicle while on the phone with a customer. I'll treasure it forever." Kat waved a sticky note.

They got
the dog!

She fiercely hugged the family and then turned her attention to the noticeably emaciated Jade.

"There you are, you beautiful little girl." Kat knelt and petted Jade. "Whitney Bermes from the *Bozeman Daily Chronicle* is here to meet you all." Kat introduced the staff writer who stepped out of the crowd to shake hands. They arranged themselves on the green lawn of the

Mammoth Terrace Grill, while Whitney conducted the interview.

Dozens of people came to pet Jade, many exclaiming she was a "miracle dog" for having survived so long in the wilderness. Several of Kat's officemates admitted finding Jade was a needed boost to everyone's morale in Yellowstone.

While Kat caressed Jade, she told the reporter, "I was sure this girl would come to her owners, even when she hadn't been spotted for twelve days. I couldn't give up, knowing that the family was grief-stricken, as I would have been had it been one of my fur kids. They drove to Yellowstone for over ten hours each way on three different occasions, all for the love of their dog." Kat beamed. "And now Jade is going home."

Whitney recorded a video of the reunion. David sat on the ground, his braced leg stretched out in front of him, wearing his *Only the Strong Survive Yellowstone* shirt. Angie sat grinning behind him, with Jade securely leashed. David, in his Texan drawl, gave his account of Jade's recovery that morning.

"I didn't believe Laura at first." He grinned widely. "But it was true!"

He recalled the times he'd almost given up, his despair, and then the encouragement Kat had given them. Jade wiggled her bottom. "Girl, I'm not going anywhere, I promise. You and I are going to stick together."

When David thanked Whitney for the interview, she replied, "It's my pleasure to report such happy news. This is a once-in-a-lifetime story."

After the reporter left, Kat showed David her phone. "Look at this. Jade's famous."

David stared at the flood of Facebook posts on *Bring Jade Home* filled with congratulations. Thousands of people were praising everyone involved in recovering his dog. There were enough contributions to David's GoFundMe page to cover much of his travel costs.

David swiped at his eyes and turned toward Kat. "I want you to have the reward. We couldn't have found her without you."

Kat shook her head. "No way." She insisted that the volunteers, especially Kevin Torphy, who spent over sixty hours searching for Jade, were the true heroes, giving their spare time and energy to search for Jade. There were also the long-distance angels who sent encouragement, helpful ideas, and most importantly to Kat, their prayers.

Laura chimed in. "David and I already agreed I would match his reward. If you won't take it, maybe we could donate it?"

"Then the National Wolfwatcher Coalition is my choice." Kat smiled at them. "This is one of the best days of my life."

David gave Jade a light pat on the head. "Me too, Kat. Me too."

Back at Canyon Village the family and Kat gathered around the fire pit sipping Champagne from plastic glasses, while rangers, employees, and visitors came by to congratulate them. One ranger suggested they rename Jade "Everts" in honor of the man lost for thirty-seven days in Yellowstone.

Kat pointed a few hundred yards away. "Better yet, I think that should be called 'Jade's Meadow.'"

Patti Johnson had called David earlier, wanting to know if the rumor was true, and he invited her to the party to see for herself. When she arrived, she handed David a large, yellow object. "I knew exactly where I'd left Tweety in the meadow."

David admitted it was an unusual toy. He set it in front of Jade. She regarded it suspiciously, and he roared with laughter. Fortunately, Patti also had two huge marrowbones for each of the dogs, which they chewed together, buddies again.

David beamed. "Here she is, in living color."

Patti knelt to pet her, and then displayed two of Jade's flyers. One was unmarked; the other had handwritten search updates scrawled across it. "I'm going to keep them as souvenirs."

Laura said, "I think I'll take one down and have it framed for David."

His throat tightened as he studied the marked-up flyer, a graphic history of the last six weeks. "I'd like that."

When Kevin Torphy and his wife, Elena, arrived, Kat introduced them to the family. Jade lounged at David's feet. "Without Kevin, we wouldn't be here celebrating."

The tall man knelt and petted Jade gently, as if he knew she was fragile.

"This lass is a might thin isn't she? But healthy otherwise." Kevin stood, and shook David's good hand. "You are a lucky man, sir. I'm pleased to meet you."

"I am very lucky. I heard you played my call a...bit."

"More than a little. I still hear it in my sleep." Kevin did an imitation of David's voice and whistle, causing Jade to perk her ears forward. Everyone gathered laughed, complimenting him on the accuracy of the call.

After the laughter died down, David gripped Kevin's hand. "Thanks, man."

Kevin shrugged. "I would've wanted someone to do the same for me."

The sun cast deep shadows, and the sky glowed orange toward the west. The wind rustled the aspens, their leaves turning over gold. Wood smoke from fireplaces hung in the air. They were coming up on winter, and David realized Jade had returned to Laura just in time.

As if reading his mind, Kat rubbed her arms. "Snow's coming soon. I was concerned with Canyon closing down shortly we'd have a lot less chance of seeing her."

David said, "When I was sitting in the meadow, sometimes I had the sensation Jade was in the woods, watching us."

Kat nodded. "She may have been enjoying her freedom in the wilderness, but still keeping an eye on you."

"But wouldn't the wolves or the bears hunt her?" Angie asked.

"If any animal might harm her it would be coyotes. I was less worried about the wolves. The mothers love puppies because all summer they secrete oxytocin, the love hormone, after they give birth and nurse."

"So they saw Jade as a wolf puppy? How cool!" Angie smiled.

"Basically yes." Kat laughed. "That's why the wolves tolerate annoying pups biting their ears and tails. Why wouldn't they accept Jade?"

"Parents do put up with a lot." David grinned at Angie, who made a face back at him. "But Kat, why do you think she ended up at Canyon? Because my SUV was there?"

"She may have smelled it. Maybe she was attracted to all the people around her, and torn between freedom and security."

Laura said, "Don't you think she was in full survival mode?"

"Still, she seemed to remember people were a source of love, food, and comfort. Otherwise, she could have gone into the backcountry, never to be found. Instead, she chose to stay here." Kat relayed the story of the raven, flying directly in front of her car. "I had asked for a sign to focus the search for Jade. The bird took me to the meadow, but I missed the message."

Laura raised her brows. "Now that you mention it, I did see a raven out of the corner of my eye flying over Jade this morning."

"Do you think it was blind luck Jade came to you?"

Laura shrugged. "I don't know. Maybe she recognized Laila's bark."

"That could be." Kat gazed up at the stars beginning to define themselves in the darkening sky. "Or maybe, you needed good news from the Universe more than anyone."

David doubted Kat's last theories, but politely resisted saying anything. He was the son of a scientist who believed in rational explanations and proof. Maybe the raven had just been flying to avoid Kat's truck. Jade may very well have come in to Laura just for treats, since she was obviously hungry.

The party moved indoors to their warmer cabin. Patti had taken on the role of photographer, recording the evening with hundreds of images. David noticed the fatigue on Laura and Angie as their adrenaline waned. His knee ached after standing on it too much. He knew he had at least one more surgery ahead of him, and dreaded the thought. David watched as Jade's head lowered.

After an hour or so, their new friends said their goodbyes. Patti offered to follow Kat home since her truck was still not running properly.

"I'm fine," Kat insisted. "Once it starts, I'm good."

"And you're driving in the dark. What about all those animals?" Laura frowned.

Kat laughed. "Believe me, I'm used to it. I've never had a problem."

It struck David that all of them had long drives ahead. They had all made the round trip to Canyon countless times to find his pup.

Ready for sleep, Jade was draped across David's chest, her head nestled in the crook of his arm. She had run back and forth between the beds, jumping on Angie and then on him until she finally settled with David. He could hear Laila breathing soundly in her crate.

Laura yawned. "Are you comfortable with her like that?"

"I'm fine." Jade's slight bulk atop him was hardly a burden. She was much lighter than she had been six weeks before. He'd take her to the vet as soon as he could get an appointment, but he estimated she'd lost about half of her weight. He reached over and held Laura's hand until her breath became regular and deep.

He recalled Kat telling him earlier, "You deserved to get this girl back."

As he lay beneath Jade's warmth, David wasn't sure he deserved anything, but he was thankful for what the day had brought him.

With news of Jade's return, his son, Scott, had been overjoyed. David's disagreement with Angie was a moot point. Six weeks ago, he and Laura had been wondering if their relationship could survive a week's vacation together. Since then, she'd become a part of his life, not only taking care of him, but bringing Jade in. For the first time in years, he had hope for a close relationship with a woman, built on trust, friendship, and the intimacy of shared experiences.

He ran his hand gently over Jade's still-glossy fur. From the beginning, he had described her as "independent." She seemed to regard David as a peer, so intelligent that she routinely questioned his commands, and decided on an individual basis whether to obey them.

David recalled the look in Jade's eyes this morning before she leapt toward him. There had been something different in her expression, beyond the questioning he so often read. He was struck with the hypothesis that she had been at war between her desire for freedom and her feelings for him. Today, he'd recognized the emotion in her blue gaze he could only identify as love.

He replayed Kat's theories, pondering whether or not they could be true. With a chill, he remembered the shadow of a raven crossing over him when he stood, whistling for Jade before she appeared and then ran away. If it was true the world could possibly give people what they needed most, then for him, it was Jade: independent, smart, tough, and the ultimate survivor.

Jade stretched one leg against his arm, and let out a long sigh. David's eyes grew heavier, and he too sighed with contentment. He wasn't sure what the repercussions from Jade's experiences would be, and he had a long road of recovery ahead of him.

They had both survived disaster and had been given another chance. It was going to be hard work, but they would heal together, starting tomorrow when David would bring Jade home.

Chapter Twenty-two

THE MIRACLE DOG

"Animals are the bridge between us and the beauty of all that is natural. They show us what's missing in our lives, and how to love ourselves more completely and unconditionally. They connect us back to who we are, and to the purpose of why we're here."
—Trisha McCagh

Bring Jade Home · September 5 · Bring Jade Home As Admin of this page I get to see statistics and let me tell you....we have reached over 200,000 people! So Jade, you might be the most famous dog out there right now!!! Thank you to everyone who had their heart in this adventure we have all been on for 44 days! All it took was a lot of prayers, good wishes, a lot of Hope and Diligence to BRING JADE HOME! Thank you all, With love and respect...Sandy Monville.

SEPTEMBER 5: David turned to Angie, who rode in the back seat where

Jade slept on her lap.

"Better wake up Marilyn Monroe. Her adoring public awaits," David joked.

An NBC Denver news crew milled in his driveway. Jade didn't appear impressed. Instead, she gave a big yawn as Angie fastened her lead.

"I guess we're going to have to learn to live with a star." Laura grinned. She'd been on the phone with Sandy Monville, the *Bring Jade Home* Facebook administrator, for most of the trip from Yellowstone. They'd fielded questions from local and national reporters. Someone had labeled Jade "The Miracle Dog," and the moniker stuck.

"I even had a voicemail from Lester Holt's assistant!" Sandy had told her.

They were all exhausted, but David did his best to tell Jade's story to the news people as he blinked under the bright lights.

Jade seemed to droop with exhaustion, and he begged off. "We've had a long day," he explained.

"I'd say you had a long forty-four days," one of the crew replied.

On the vet's metal table, Jade patiently let him examine and weigh her. She was twenty-three pounds, down from around forty.

"Well David, she's remarkably healthy." The vet gave her a pat on the head. "She's thin, of course, but everything else is good—no fleas or ticks. I didn't even find anything stuck in her fur."

"We thought she had a scab on her upper lip." David explained Angie had picked it off when grooming Jade, and decided it was either pine resin or a small piece of tar.

The vet examined the area. "No hint of a cut, let alone a scar."

"How do you think she survived over six weeks on her own?" David was still amazed.

"There was plenty of fresh water. She probably ate small mammals and animal scat. We'll deworm her, but only as a precaution." He shook his head. "Technically, she's still a puppy. Maybe the wolves saw her as a pup rather than competition." He did a quick calculation. "For her, six weeks was almost 11 percent of her life to date. She may be changed by the experience, behaviorally if not physically."

Jade cocked her head and gazed into his eyes.

The vet laughed. "She is one smart, lucky dog."

David called Jade's breeder with the good news. John Bonato was relieved she had survived Yellowstone, but told David he wasn't surprised.

"Jade's pedigree goes back to the Hartnagle's Las Rocosa Aussies. You know those black diamond ski runs in Vail? It used to be a ranch." John explained Las Rocosa Aussies could tirelessly herd cattle there in the blazing Colorado summer heat, with elevation changes of 3,400 feet. They were tough, smart, and able to handle high altitudes.

"You picked the right puppy," John added. "There's a good chance no other breed would've made it."

A few days later, a limo picked up the family and delivered them to the local FOX TV news station. Jade had recovered much of her energy as she walked beside David down the studio hallway before the broadcast. She suddenly pulled on her leash and squatted.

"Oh no." David's face flushed.

Station employees scrambled to clean up the pile, reassuring him it was "normal for animal segments."

After his interview, Laura told David he appeared remarkably calm.

"I was nervous as hell. But then, I saw Jade sitting there, and it was so good to tell the story." He bent and patted her head.

His Aussie shook her rear, and licked his hand.

Laura was excited to take part in Denver's CBS segment, "Vets urge extra precautions when traveling with pets." All of her life, seeing dogs in the back of pickups, on their owners' laps, or hanging out car windows, she had wanted to promote travel safety for animal companions.

When dog lovers objected to using harnesses or crates—"They're our family. We can't contain them!"—Laura would counter, "We use safety belts and carriers for our children, why not our pets?"

"Never let your dog ride without proper protection," Laura advised in the segment. "At only thirty miles an hour, a pet can become a missile, injuring you and themselves. Use a crate or a harness approved by the Center for Pet Safety."

The news team filmed the couple, who spoke of the accident, describing Jade's carrier after the impact. The Aussies adroitly jumped on command into the back of the SUV with its secured carriers. The piece ended with a close-up of Jade's blue eyes staring into the camera though the wire of her crate. Laura stated, "No one wants to go through the heartbreak we did."

Laura posted the segment on the *Bring Jade Home* Facebook page. Many followers responded, vowing to consider more protection for their beloved dogs while driving.

Laura resumed agility judging, traveling the continental United States. On the last day of a competition in Alaska, she shared Jade's story with the participants, many shedding first tears of concern, then joy. One woman told Laura that while visiting her daughter in Yellowstone, she too had searched for Jade.

Laura hugged the woman, thanking her for all her efforts. Jade's dilemma had tapped the good in so many people, and united them in a common cause of caring and survival. She and David might never be able to express their gratitude to every one of them, but she would try to do so whenever she could.

A few nights later, David was on the couch with his leg propped up and Jade on his lap. When he flipped the channel to a National Geographic wildlife special, Jade leapt off the sofa and ran toward the television where a grizzly bear loped across an open field. She barked and yelped in a high pitch. She quieted whenever the camera focused strictly on scenery. Then, when a wolf pack sprinted across the screen, she ran with them, yipping furiously until they disappeared.

A chill ran through David. Jade *knew* these animals.

"She never did this before," he said as Laura videoed the frantic dog running at the flat-screen TV. At some point in her Yellowstone journey, Jade had likely encountered bears, both black and grizzly, on her route from Norris to Canyon. She may have crossed paths with other animals along the power line "roadway," including coyotes and wolves, who perhaps viewed her as a puppy, a curiosity rather than a competitor.

"I'm not sure if she's afraid, or wants to run with them. But, I agree. Jade knows what they are and remembers."

David became aware of other changes in his Aussie. Jade rarely left his side. He would turn and almost trip over her she remained so close.

"I'm not leaving you, silly."

Jade fixated on him. She stopped jumping the fence and no longer visited other dogs or the kids at the nearby schoolyard.

Laura and David took Jade and Laila on their first hike together after Jade's return. The rugged Colorado mountainsides were swathed in golden aspen trees. A crisp fall breeze carried the scent of pine and decaying leaves. Gray-tinted clouds dotted the sky.

Jade tugged eagerly at her leash toward the deep pine forest around her.

Laura frowned. "You're not afraid she'll take off? Sorry, it still makes me nervous."

"Naw. It's like she's attached to me by an invisible leash."

Laura held her breath, recalling how his dog had sometimes ignored his calls in the past.

Now, however, Jade ran only a few yards ahead, stopped, and returned to David, proving his point.

Laura sighed with relief.

Jade sniffed the air, and charged to the nearby stream that bubbled over the rocks. Like the Jade of old, she jumped in splashing and swimming, apparently relishing the water as she always had. Laila followed her older friend, but only to the point where her paws were wet.

"Well, at least some things never change." Laura laughed as Jade showered them with water flying off her fur.

David, determined not to use crutches, walked slowly, and Laura matched his pace. Pausing, Jade sniffed under a stand of lodgepole pines.

Together Laila and Jade dashed ahead, playing like littermates in a mountain meadow, much like the one where Jade came to Laura.

They moved alongside the forest, the autumn sunshine shining through the pines. Then Jade stiffened, hackles raised. Her ears perked up at a sound. She dashed and returned with a mouse in her mouth. They watched as Jade chewed her prey. Laila cocked her head, as if wondering at the correlation between the small rodent and food.

"Good job, girl! You know how to hunt!" David grinned.

"That *is* a change." As the Aussie swallowed her prey, Laura saw a flash of the tough, feral dog who had survived so long against the odds. Then Jade caught her glance, wiggled her rear, and tore off ahead of them with Laila on her heels, their barks echoing off the mountains.

For dinner a few weeks later, David grilled steaks, and cooked an extra one for Jade.

"You're spoiling her. She's put on so much weight she's as broad as a coffee table," Laura joked. "We're going to have to put her on the 'Yellowstone Diet.'"

"She's still recovering," David argued.

Laura watched Jade polish off the rest of David's table scraps and plead for more.

Casting a warning look at David, Laura cleared the kitchen and they settled on the couch. Laura surveyed the scene. Her two older dogs were curled at her feet, already falling into doggie dreams. Laila munched on a bone, completely absorbed in her task. Jade centered herself on the couch, bookended by David and Laura.

Jade first turned her full attention toward David, whose eyes were already closing. She then scanned the room, alert. Laura reached over and petted the Aussie's head, letting her know all was well.

With a sigh of contentment, Jade lay down.

"Girl, I'm putting you on a diet, starting tomorrow." Laura said softly.

"No you're not," David muttered.

Laura smiled. David would always spoil Jade. Some things would never change.

Then Jade cast her blue eyes on Laura, the connection so strong it sent chills down her arms. Perhaps, Laura thought, Jade really *was* a Miracle Dog, not only for surviving unscathed against all the odds. Jade had touched so many people in a positive way. Kat credited Jade's recovery for boosting the morale in Yellowstone after the tragedies of that summer.

People who had lost their animal companions turned to *Bring Jade Home* on Facebook for advice, sharing their triumphs and grieving their losses. Pet-lovers wrote they would transport their dogs more safely after the pet safety video post. Jade's followers had responded with thousands of well wishes, relief, and happiness for everyone concerned. Many wrote they were inspired and heartened by the tremendous efforts of people to care for animals and each other.

David was on the road to recovery with his beloved Aussie by his side. Laura herself would face the future with more confidence, knowing that Jade had trusted her in the meadow.

Laura gave Jade a final pat. "All for the love of a dog," she whispered.

⦀⦀⦀⦀⦀⦀⦀⦀⦀⦀⦀⦀ *Acknowledgments*

Laura, David, Angie, and Scott wish to thank everyone mentioned in this book, along with the many anonymous Good Samaritans who helped at the crash site and all those who generously searched for a stranger's dog. They also want to acknowledge the support of the National Park Service at Yellowstone, Xanterra Parks and Resorts, and their employees.

I wish to thank the North Naples and Bonita Springs Writers' Group: Beverly A. Jackson, Glenn Erick Miller, D.L. Williams, Robert Erickson, Margo Carey, and Jeff Bruce. Additionally, thanks to Jayden and Sana Flynn and their two dogs, Durin and Ginger, who acted as technical assistants on our Skype critique meetings. Christine DeSmet and the UW Madison Writer's Institute program helped me hone my craft.

A big thank you to my beta readers: Julie Shanahan, Jo Ann Hay, Val Nuti, Debbie Jackman, Mary McCluskey, Janet Chapple, and Beth Chapple. Your input spurred me on.

A special thanks to Will Harmon and the team at Farcountry Press for their enthusiasm for Jade's story.

My husband Paul Caffrey supported me throughout the entire process. I couldn't have undertaken this project without his backing.

Finally, I want to thank Jade's family for the opportunity to tell their uplifting story with its happy conclusion. It's been a privilege to write this book.

Michelle Caffrey

www.BringJadeHome.com
Jade's fan Facebook page: Bring Jade Home

About the Author ||||||||||||||||||||||||||

After years in the software industry, Michelle and her husband Paul abandoned successful software careers and bought a converted 1906 Dutch barge, *Imagine*. They cruised the European waterways for ten adventure-filled years, while Michelle wrote *Just Imagine: A New Life on an Old Boat*, the story of their first-year voyage from Holland to France.

Michelle and Paul now divide their time between Lake Geneva, Wisconsin, and Naples, Florida. Michelle is a member of RWA and a co-facilitator of the North Naples/Bonita Springs Writers' Group. A nature and wildlife lover, she is a volunteer Boardwalk Naturalist at Audubon's Corkscrew Swamp Sanctuary in Naples, Florida.

Jade at home in Colorado.

The accident July 23

Missing Dog - "Jade"

Missing in Yellowstone National Park

Escaped from scene of auto accident July 23

RECENT SIGHTINGS:

Between Norris Junction & Canyon Junction

* Employee Lodging area near Canyon Junction.

* Near the Construction pile, one mile from Virginia Cascades which is between Norris Junction and Canyon Junction.

* Virginia Cascades Drive toward the end of the one-way drive.

* Jade is skittish following her recent trauma. **DO NOT CHASE** her.

* If you see Jade, try to **ENTICE** her **TO YOU.** Sit quietly and allow her to approach you. She may be inclined to approach people with other dogs. Dogs must be ON LEASH at all times.

* If you see Jade, please call/text Angie - (720)935- ███ AND post your report at www.facebook.com/YellowstoneNationalParkVisitor to keep other searchers apprised.

* When recovered, Cheryl from Stop the Car Trading Post 1-406-838- ███ in Silver Gate, MT will hold her for the family.

Kat, Laura, Laila, Patti, Kevin, Angie, Jade, and David

Michelle, David, and Laura with Jade and Laila

Bibliography and Resources |||||||||||||||||||||||||

FOR MORE INFORMATION ON YELLOWSTONE NATIONAL PARK:

In the Temple of Wolves: A Winter's Immersion in Wild Yellowstone, by Rick Lamplugh

Death in Yellowstone: Accidents and Foolhardiness in the First National Park, by Lee H. Whittlesey

Lost in the Yellowstone: "Thirty-Seven Days of Peril" and a Handwritten Account of Being Lost, by Truman Everts (author) and Lee H. Whittlesey (editor)

Yellowstone Treasures: The Traveler's Companion to the National Park, by Janet Chapple

National Park Service Yellowstone
https://www.nps.gov/yell

The National Parks: America's Best Idea. Six-episode series produced by Ken Burns and Dayton Duncan and written by Dayton Duncan. http://www.pbs.org/nationalparks/

MEDIA FEATURING JADE:

- *Bozeman Daily Chronicle*
- KUSA, NBC Denver
- FOX news
- People.com
- *The Guardian, United Kingdom*
- CBS 2 Denver

PET SAFETY: The Center for Pet Safety is a registered 501(c)(3) non-profit research and consumer advocacy organization dedicated to companion animal and consumer safety.

http://www.centerforpetsafety.org/

FOR INFORMATION ON AUSTRALIAN SHEPHERDS:

The American Kennel Club breed information
http://www.akc.org/dog-breeds/australian-shepherd/

The Australian Shepherd Club of America
http://www.asca.org

Hartnagle's Las Rocosa Aussies
http://www.lasrocosa.com/5280joshdean.html

Jade's breeder, Bonato Aussies
http://australianshepherdcolorado.com/index.php

Discussion Questions ||||||||||||||||||||||||

- Did you enjoy the book? If so, what stood out? If not, why not?

- Were you engaged immediately, or did it take you a while to get into it?

- Besides Jade, who did you feel the most empathy towards?

- What major emotional responses did the story evoke in you?

- Did the book take you outside your comfort zone?

- What main themes does the book explore?

- The accident and its aftermath tested Laura and David's early relationship. How would the story's impact differ had their friendship simply petered out?

- How do you think Kat's determination affected the outcome?

- What did you think of the people involved? Was it important to like or admire them?

- Were there any people you loved to hate?

- Why did they do what they did? Were their actions justified?

- Did anyone in the story remind you of people you know?

- Did Jade's plight change the people involved? If so, how?

- Laura had been in the role of caregiver for years. How do you think this influenced her relationship with David when he was injured?

- How is David's approach to life different from Kat's?

- How effective were the social media quotes as a clue for personality?

- The setting of Yellowstone National Park is integral to the story. Which of the challenges Jade faced in the wilderness impressed you the most?

- Yellowstone has been called a "Dangerous Beauty." How did reading about the dark side of the park make you feel?

- Did you learn anything new about the park and the people there? Has the book inspired you to visit Yellowstone or other national parks?

- Kat Brekken is passionate about protecting wildlife, especially grizzles and wolves. Do you agree or disagree with her perspective? Why?

- Ecological issues are increasingly important in our world. Did this book make you aware of people's negative impact on the environment? Are wildlife and our parks worth protecting?

- What do you think about the way Laura handled her moral dilemma? Should people whose spouses are victims of advanced Alzheimer's and dementia "become a second casualty to the disease"? Did her situation trigger any conversations with your own spouse or partner?

- The death of Lance Crosby resulted in a mother grizzly being euthanized. This was a difficult and complex decision. If the decision had been yours to make, what would you have done? How did you feel about the decision to send the cubs to a zoo rather than a wildlife rehabilitation center?

- Should David have put the recovery of Jade above his responsibilities and health? What do you think of his priorities?

- When Jade ran from David, he felt "It was as useless as waving steak and meatballs in the air if Jade refused to come to him." How did you feel about David's level of despair when you read it?

- After Jade runs from David, he tells Laura, "You don't know what it's like to see someone you love, and they don't recognize you." When she responds that she does know, what did you think?

- When Laura guesses Jade came to her because of Laila's bark, Kat replies, "That could be. Or maybe, you needed good news from the Universe more than anyone." Why do *you* think Jade came to Laura and not anyone else?

- Were there any other passages that struck you in particular?

- Were you satisfied with the book's ending? Would you have enjoyed the book if the ending hadn't been a happy one?

- What do you think the future holds for David, Laura, and Jade?

- Did the book leave any questions open-ended that you would like to know the answer to?

- What do you think Jade's legacy will be? Will people think differently about how they transport their pets?

- Had you read reviews before reading the book? If so, did you agree with the reviewers or not?

- If you had to halve the size of your book collection, would this book stay or go?

- If you could ask the author a question, what would it be?